ADVANCE PRAISE

"Ryan Minton's *Uplifted* beautifully demonstrates that the most powerful leadership isn't about authority—it's about appreciation, presence, and service. His stories and strategies will equip you to create a culture where your team feels valued, energized, and ready to deliver exceptional experiences. This book will change how you lead—and impact those you lead."

—Jon Gordon, 17x best-selling author of
The Power of Positive Leadership
and The Energy Bus

"Ryan Minton is the real deal. With twenty years in hospitality, he knows that exceptional customer experiences start with great leadership. In this book, he shares a proven roadmap for building a culture that empowers frontline employees to create unforgettable, loyalty-driving moments."

—Shep Hyken, customer service/CX expert
and New York Times *best-selling author*

"Of the many reasons to like this book, two stand out. First, the author isn't just a theorist—he's a proven practitioner with the experience to back up his insights. Second, the content is highly practical, not abstract. Ryan delivers so many great ideas that your biggest challenge will be choosing which to implement first. I highly recommend it."

—Mark Sanborn, award-winning speaker
and author of The Fred Factor

"In *Uplifted: The Remarkable Power of Positive Leadership on Frontline Teams*, Ryan Minton provides compelling examples of how small, consistent actions of appreciation and positivity lead to increased employee engagement, customer satisfaction, and organizational success. In addition to being inspirational, *Uplifted* is actionable, offering specific strategies to foster a positive workplace culture that thrives even during challenging times. For anyone leading a team, *Uplifted* is the essential guide to creating environments where people feel valued, empowered, and motivated."

—Joseph Michelli, PhD, New York Times *#1*
best-selling author of books like The Starbucks
Experience *and* The New Gold Standard

"In the competitive restaurant industry, the difference between success and failure often comes down to leadership. Ryan Minton's *Uplifted* offers invaluable insights into creating the kind of positive team environment where exceptional service naturally flourishes. His strategies have helped us elevate both team engagement and guest experiences across our IHOP locations."

–Larry Brakefield, president of Sunshine
Restaurant Partners, IHOP's largest franchisee

"In *Uplifted*, Ryan Minton so beautifully captures a lesson I learned while building my first company, Student Maid—that extraordinary results come from leaders who prioritize the growth of their people over the pursuit of perfection. His practical framework revolutionizes service delivery by first creating environments where teams feel empowered to learn from their mistakes, have the confidence to take ownership, and feel safe to be human. I wish I had read this book when I started my business. A must-read for leaders who understand that investing in their people is the top priority . . . and is the key to building a business that stands out from the rest."

–Kristen Hadeed, author
of Permission to Screw Up

"YES! Ryan Minton's book is a must-read for any leader who wants to empower their team, lead from the heart, and create a thriving culture of positivity. His real-world experiences and actionable strategies remind us that leadership isn't about power—it's about people. I love how Ryan brings to life the simple yet powerful ways we can make our teams feel valued, confident, and inspired to deliver amazing experiences. If you're ready to step up, say YES to positive leadership, and create a workplace where people love to show up and shine, this book is for you!"

–Christine Trippi, author of Yes Is the
Answer *and founder of The Wise Pineapple*

Uplifted

Uplifted

The Remarkable Power
of Positive Leadership
on Frontline Teams

RYAN MINTON

UPLIFTED
The Remarkable Power of Positive Leadership on Frontline Teams

Copyright © 2025 by Ryan Minton

Disclaimer: This book has been published for the purpose of providing the reader with general information on its subject matter. The author and the publisher believe the information to be accurate and authoritative at the time of publication. The book is sold with the understanding that neither the author nor the publisher is providing professional advice, and the reader should not rely upon this book as such. Every situation is different, and professional advice (whether psychological, legal, financial, tax, or otherwise) should only be obtained from a professional licensed in your jurisdiction who has knowledge of the specific facts and circumstances.

Book Cover Design by Abigael Elliott
Interior Layout and Design by Stephanie Anderson
Editorial Team: Jim Sloan, Chloie Benton, Annika Bergen

ISBNs:
979-8-89165-263-7 *Paperback*
979-8-89165-264-4 *Hardback*
979-8-89165-262-0 *E-book*

Published by:
Streamline Books
Kansas City, MO
streamlinebookspublishing.com

Streamline
BOOKS

To my Radiator Springs crew: Charlie, whose smile shines brighter than any trophy, and Tressa, who makes our family road trip perfect every single day.

CONTENTS

FOREWORD

I bet you still remember the best boss you've ever had.

Their name, their impact, the way they made you *feel*—those things stay with you. Great bosses, like great teachers, leave an indelible mark on our lives. They inspire us to be better versions of ourselves and help us unlock skills we didn't even know we possessed.

In short, they make us feel *uplifted*.

Now, contrast that with the memory of the worst boss you've ever had.

Just as our best bosses leave a lasting impression, so do the worst ones—but for entirely different reasons.

Chances are, you can still recall—in vivid detail—some of their most awful traits. Just the memory of them may elicit a physical reaction. Did you recoil in disgust or anger when you pictured them?

You likely weren't inspired to do your best work while you were on their team. In fact, you may have spent more time plotting your escape from the situation than thinking about how to perform well in that role.

Great businesses aren't built by chance—they're built by people.

The best leaders know this. They understand that thriving organizations are fueled not just by strategy, innovation, or even customer loyalty but by the passion, dedication, and engagement of the employees who fulfill customer promises every day.

Happy employees create happy customers, and happy customers create successful businesses. It's a simple equation, yet one that too many leaders overlook. And, while many facets of business are changing at a rapid pace, this truism will remain unchanged.

That's why I'm so thrilled to lend my enthusiastic endorsement to the book you're holding. Ryan Minton is one of the best leaders I know. You don't have to spend much time with him to figure out that "policy" is one of his least favorite words. It takes even less time to realize that another "P" word—"people"—is his favorite. His face lights up every time he has the opportunity to brag about the qualities of his employees, past and present.

Ryan Minton has spent his career mastering both the art and science of exceptional leadership. With a deep background in hospitality and customer experience, he's seen firsthand how the best companies don't just serve their customers well—they take care of their employees first.

And, while "take care of your people so they take care of your customers" might sound obvious, it's a lesson many leaders are doomed to relearn again and again because they lack a predictable, repeatable system for prioritizing employee experience.

In the pages that follow, Ryan puts forward exactly that: a powerful, people-first approach to leadership that can radically transform any workplace into one where employees feel appreciated, supported, and empowered to make the business *better*. He offers a guide for not just recognizing the efforts and contributions of employees but also making them feel appreciated for who they are *beyond* their job descriptions as well.

My favorite element of this book is best summarized in a third "P": practicality. Ryan isn't preaching about the virtues of leadership in a theoretical, academic sense; he's sharing firsthand stories about real-world situations, making the takeaways both immediate and actionable. You aren't just reading about what *could* be if your employees were engaged; you're given the step-by-step blueprint for building an environment where they truly are.

I've spent nearly two decades studying what turns customers into superfans, and I can tell you unequivocally that your customers won't love your brand if your employees don't love it first. Apathetic employees create apathetic customers, while engaged employees create loyal advocates who return again and again.

Whether you're a CEO, a mid-level manager, or someone who—like me—was thrust into your first leadership role with zero training or guidance, this book will make you better. Not just a better *leader*, but a better employee, too. You'll walk away inspired to make your team feel more valued, supported, and motivated every day.

Being placed in a leadership role is truly a gift. Just think: one day, when a member of your team is asked to recall the boss who most shaped their career or touched their lives, they might just share a story about *you*. And, whether that story takes place after a major event or on a random Tuesday, its ripple effects will continue to be felt for much longer than you might imagine.

As you read this book, don't just absorb the insights—act on them. When you reach the reflection questions, don't rush through them. Instead, challenge yourself to set a concrete, time-bound action for each one. Leadership doesn't happen in theory; it happens in the trenches.

No, go forward and uplift—you've got this!

Brittany Hodak, customer experience speaker,
creator of the SUPER framework,
Shark Tank *success story,*
and author of Creating Superfans:
How to Turn Your Customers Into Lifelong Advocates

PREFACE

Hey there! Before we jump into all the exciting principles of positive leadership, I'd love to give you a quick win right from the start. I've put together a super-quick Positive Leadership Assessment that you can complete in under ninety seconds.

This assessment will show you exactly where you are on your leadership journey right now. Think of it as taking a quick selfie of your leadership mindset before we explore these concepts together!

Head over to ryanminton.com/leader to get your baseline score. Having this perspective will make your experience so much more valuable as you dive into all the fantastic ideas and principles we'll be exploring throughout this book.

A Journey of Positive Leadership

I never planned on being an author or keynote speaker. In fact, if you had told me years ago, when I was first starting out as a teenager working at a theme park, that I'd one day be traveling the world sharing leadership insights, I probably would have laughed. But life has a funny way of leading us down unexpected paths, especially when we're open to learning and growth.

My journey into the world of leadership began in an unexpected place: a theme park in Cincinnati called Kings Island. Throughout high school and college, I spent my summers there, and it was in this vibrant, fast-paced environment that I first encountered the stark contrast between positive and negative leadership.

During my first summer at Kings Island, I had the opportunity to work under two very different supervisors. The first, whom we'll call James, was known for his harsh, intimidating style. He actually bragged about how many employees he could make cry in a single shift. His leadership, if you could call it that, was built on fear and intimidation.

Then there was Stephanie. She was everything James wasn't—positive, encouraging, and invested in her team's success. Stephanie saw something in the quiet, awkward teenager that I was and found ways to bring out the best in me. And it wasn't just me—she had this incredible ability to inspire and motivate everyone around her.

The difference between these two leadership styles was like night and day. Under James, we worked because we had to, constantly looking over our shoulders and dreading our shifts. But with Stephanie, we were excited to come to work. We felt valued, supported, and motivated to give our best.

It was during that summer that I made a decision that went on to shape my entire career: I wanted to be like Stephanie. I wanted to lead in a way that brought out the best in people, that made them feel valued, and that inspired them to excel.

This early experience in the service industry shaped my entire approach to leadership. Research shows that, like me, up to one-third of Americans start their careers in service jobs—in restaurants, hotels, retail stores, and other customer-facing roles. As leaders in these industries, we often have the privilege of being someone's first "boss." It's a big responsibility. We can shape their perception of work and leadership and influence their career trajectory for years to come. A great leader can spark confidence in a new employee by seeking and listening to their input and challenging them to learn and grow. However, a negative leader can discourage a first-time employee through constant criticism and micromanagement, leaving scars of self-doubt. These early experiences often become the lens through which employees view their professional journey. Luckily, Stephanie's influence was more impactful on me than James' was.

In the years since then, my journey in the hospitality industry took me from working the front desk of a Cincinnati hotel to being senior vice president of one of the most respected hotel management companies in the industry. I've had the privilege of working with industry giants like Hilton and Marriott, experiencing firsthand the challenges and triumphs of leading large teams in high-pressure environments.

But this book isn't about my career path or my achievements. It's about how positive leadership transforms not just businesses, but lives.

I've worked with some incredible people—from housekeepers and bellhops to executives and owners. I've seen how great leaders transform struggling properties into success stories, disengaged employees into passionate team members, and ordinary customer experiences into extraordinary ones.

My teams have transformed floundering hotels into market and brand leaders. But the real success wasn't in the improved metrics or the awards (though those were nice). The real success was in the changed lives—the employees who rediscovered their passion for their work, the guests who felt cared for, and the teams that came together to achieve what seemed impossible.

These experiences taught me something crucial: employees who feel like they matter make customers feel like they matter. It's a simple concept, but one that's often overlooked in the hustle and bustle of daily operations and the pressure to meet financial targets.

That's why I'm on a mission to make the front-line employee experience better, not just in the hospitality industry, but across all industries, around the world. Because I've seen how powerful it can be when people feel valued, appreciated, and empowered in their work.

In this book, we're going to explore the principles of positive leadership that I've seen transform organizations and lives. We'll delve into real-world examples, practical strategies, and the mindset shifts necessary to create work environments where both employees and customers thrive. Although I spent most of my career in hospitality, I've come to learn that these concepts apply across the board; if you're leading a team, this book is for you.

I was speaking at the world's largest customer contact conference in Las Vegas when an audience member approached me during the break. He shared how he'd implemented the Thanks for Coming In Today® principle I'd discussed in my previous book. His voice filled with pride as he described how this simple practice had transformed his team's morale.

"The funny thing is," he told me, "I was skeptical at first. I thought call centers are so different from hospitality. But people are people, regardless of industry." These are the stories that fuel my passion for sharing these principles through speaking and consulting—seeing how universal they truly are.

In the coming pages, you'll read about people like Jason, whose simple act of gratitude became the cornerstone of a leadership philosophy. You'll learn about the "No Bad Day Policy" and how it can revolutionize your team's morale. We'll discuss the importance of being present as a leader, of fostering diversity, and of communication that inspires and motivates.

But this isn't just a book of theories or feel-good stories. It's a practical guide, born out of years of experience in the trenches of one of the most people-focused industries out there. The strategies and principles we'll discuss have been tested in the real world, in situations ranging from daily operations to crisis management.

Whether you're a seasoned executive, a middle manager, or someone just starting out on your leadership journey, my hope is that you'll find valuable insights and actionable strategies in these pages.

Because leadership isn't about titles or positions—it's about how we interact with people, how we make them feel, and how we inspire them to be their best selves.

As we embark on this journey together, I want you to know that this book is as much about you and your potential as a leader as it is about my experiences. My goal is not to tell you what to do, but to share what I've learned, to challenge you to think differently about leadership, and to inspire you to create positive change in your own sphere of influence.

So, are you ready to explore the transformative power of positive leadership? Are you ready to discover how small changes in your approach can create ripple effects of positivity throughout your organization? Are you ready to be the kind of leader who doesn't just manage, but inspires?

If so, then let's begin. Because the world needs more positive leaders, and that journey starts right here, right now, with you.

CHAPTER 1

The Power of Positive Leadership: Jason's Legacy

In my first book, *Thanks for Coming In Today*, I share a story that has become fundamental to my philosophy of leadership. It's a story I often revisit, not just because it profoundly shaped my approach to management, but because it continues to resonate with people in powerful ways.

The story centers on a young man named Jason, a college student studying hospitality who worked as a front desk agent at a hotel I managed in Cincinnati, Ohio. From the moment he started, there was something special about him—a warmth and enthusiasm that were impossible to ignore.

Jason had a gift for making people feel valued and appreciated. His signature gesture was greeting everyone—staff and guests alike—with a warm handshake and a heartfelt, "Thanks for coming in today." But it wasn't just the words; it was the way he said them. When Jason thanked you for coming in, you felt like you made his day better. Even though I was his manager, he made me feel valued in a way I'd never experienced before. This young man, still in college, taught me one of the most profound lessons of my career: at our core, we all want to feel like we matter.

Think about that for a moment. Whether you're the CEO or the newest hire, whether you've been with a company for twenty years or twenty minutes, the basic human desire to feel appreciated, to feel like your presence makes a difference, never goes away. When Jason thanked people for coming in, he wasn't just being polite—he was acknowledging their choice to be there, their contribution to a shared purpose.

I found myself looking forward to those morning interactions with Jason. Even on the toughest days, his sincere appreciation reminded me that what we did mattered, that each of us played a vital role in our hotel's success. It was a simple thing, really—just a few words—but isn't that often where the most powerful truths lie?

One morning I watched as Jason interacted with an especially grumpy guest. This guest had been complaining about everything since he arrived—the room was too cold, the TV didn't have the channels he wanted, the coffee in the lobby wasn't strong enough. As the guest approached the front desk, looking ready to launch into another tirade, Jason intercepted him.

"Good morning, sir!" Jason said, extending his hand. "Thanks for coming in today. I hope you're having a great stay with us."

His scowl softened, and he actually shook Jason's hand. "Well, it's been okay," he mumbled, but the edge was gone from his voice.

Jason didn't stop there. He asked the guest about his trip and recommended local restaurants. By the time the guest left the lobby, he was smiling and thanking Jason for his help.

What struck me most about Jason's approach was its genuine sincerity. Here was someone who understood the power of appreciation.

He recognized that everyone, whether an employee or a customer, had made a choice to be there. Jason's simple act of acknowledgment made people feel seen and valued.

Jason brought the same positivity to his interactions with his co-workers. He greeted the housekeeping staff by name each morning, asking about their families or remembering details from previous conversations. He helped other departments during busy times, always with a smile and a word of encouragement.

One hectic day during a large convention, the entire staff was stressed, running around trying to manage the influx of guests. In the midst of this chaos, I saw Jason pull aside Sarah, a new house-keeper who was looking overwhelmed. He spoke to her quietly for a moment, and I saw her shoulders relax, a smile spreading across her face. Later, I asked Jason what he'd said to her.

"Oh, I just reminded her that she's doing a great job," he said with a shrug. "I told her that days like this are tough, but they're also when we have the biggest impact on our guests' experience. I wanted her to know that her work really matters."

That was Jason in a nutshell—always aware of the people around him, always ready with a word of encouragement or appreciation. His positivity was infectious, spreading throughout the staff and to our guests.

Tragically, Jason's life was cut short in a car accident a few years later. The loss was devastating to our entire team. But even in his passing, Jason left us with a powerful legacy.

After Jason's passing, I decided to carry on his tradition of greeting everyone with gratitude and appreciation throughout my career. It wasn't always easy—there were days when I was stressed or tired, when saying "Thanks for coming in today" felt like an effort. But I pushed through, knowing the impact it could have.

As I progressed in my career, leading different hotels across the country, I introduced Jason's greeting at each new property. Time and again, I witnessed remarkable transformations. At every hotel I managed, the culture began to shift. Staff members naturally adopted the greeting as their own. Front desk agents warmly thanked guests for choosing their hotel. Housekeepers and maintenance staff greeted each other with genuine smiles and words of appreciation.

The results were consistent across properties. Customer satisfaction scores climbed. Employee turnover dropped. Each hotel developed that same tangible positive energy that guests frequently mentioned in their reviews. This transformation was perfectly captured in a voicemail I still treasure today—from a Marriott guest who stayed over a hundred nights annually across the brand's properties. He called specifically to say he'd experienced the best stay of his travels and could sense how friendly and engaged our staff was. His words still resonate: "All hotels for me tend to run together, but yours stuck out." He urged us to continue whatever we were doing that made such a distinctive impression.

But the impact went beyond reviews, metrics, and scores. Across different properties and teams, I saw the same pattern: team members became more confident, more engaged in their work. Guests visibly relaxed, enjoying their stay more. It was as if Jason's spirit of positivity and appreciation had the power to transform any workplace where it was introduced, continuing to grow and flourish in each new setting.

What's remarkable is how Jason's story continues to resonate. As I travel across the country delivering keynote speeches to companies in various industries, I'm continually amazed by the power this simple story holds.

I've shared Jason's legacy with healthcare organizations, franchise restaurant groups, hospitality and retail teams, and industry associations. Despite the differences in these sectors, the response is always the same—a mix of inspiration and resonance.

After speaking at a large restaurant franchise conference, I had a CEO approach me, visibly moved. "We've been so focused on metrics and performance," he said, "that we've forgotten the power of simple human connection. Jason's story has reminded us of what truly matters in leadership."

At a healthcare conference, a nurse manager shared how the story inspired her to implement a similar greeting in her department. "In our rush to provide medical care, we sometimes forget the emotional needs of our patients," she explained. "Now, we make sure to greet each patient with genuine appreciation. The change in the atmosphere of our ward has been remarkable."

Even in high-pressure environments like tech startups, Jason's story strikes a chord. A young entrepreneur told me how he's using the "Thanks for coming in today" greeting to build a positive culture in his fledgling company. "In the start-up world, it's easy to get caught up in the grind," he said. "This simple practice helps us remember to appreciate each other and our shared mission."

These stories of impact underscore a fundamental truth about leadership: small, consistent actions can create monumental change. Jason's legacy isn't just about a greeting—it's about the transformative power of genuine appreciation and positive leadership.

Jason's story tells us a lot about the power of a positive attitude, but this kind of upbeat, grateful demeanor must start with those that are managing our teams. Leaders must model Jason in a way that changes how their staff thinks and feels. Only then will an appreciative attitude spread, reducing turnover, motivating staff members, and trickling down to customers in a way that brings measurable (and immeasurable!) benefits to your company.

As we delve deeper into the principles of positive leadership throughout this book, we'll explore how seemingly small gestures like Jason's can influence everything from employee engagement to customer satisfaction. We'll examine how positive leaders can cultivate environments where people feel valued, empowered, and motivated to give their best.

Jason's story serves as a powerful reminder that at its core, leadership isn't about titles or authority—it's about how we make people feel. It's about creating an environment where everyone, from the newest entry-level employee to the most loyal customer, feels appreciated and valued.

In the chapters that follow, we'll explore various aspects of positive leadership, providing practical strategies and real-world examples of how to implement these principles in your own organization. We'll discuss how to create a culture of appreciation, how to empower your team, and how to lead with empathy and authenticity.

As we embark on this journey together, I encourage you to keep Jason's story in mind. Let it serve as a reminder of the incredible impact we can have as leaders when we choose to lead with positivity, gratitude, and genuine care for others. Because in the end, that's what positive leadership is all about—positivity that can transform not just our workplaces, but the lives of everyone we touch.

Reflection Question: What simple daily practice could you implement, like Jason's "Thanks for coming in today," that would make your team members feel valued and appreciated?

CHAPTER 2

The Privilege of Leadership: Shaping Lives Through Mindful Influence

One day early in my career as a general manager, I was feeling overwhelmed by the responsibilities of running a hotel. It was 7:30 at night and I was closing the door to my office when I ran into Maria, one of our housekeepers. I'd been working since 7:00 a.m., wrestling with budgets, staffing issues, and guest complaints. Two cooks had called in sick, and the computer system had gone down for two hours during our busiest check-in period. I was exhausted and on edge, but Maria was just starting her shift and greeted me with a warm smile. "Heading home, Mr. Ryan?" she asked. "You work too hard. Make sure you get some rest."

I was struck by her genuine concern. Here was someone who worked tirelessly to keep our hotel spotless, often in thankless conditions, yet she was worried about me. It made me pause and reflect on the impact I had on the lives of my team members.

That's when it hit me: being a leader isn't just a job title or a set of responsibilities. It's a privilege—one that comes with the power to significantly impact the lives of the people we lead.

As leaders, we have the privilege of influencing how our team members spend eight to ten hours of their day, five days a week. That's more waking hours than they spend with their families. We have the power to make those hours fulfilling and growth-oriented—or stressful and unfulfilling.

This realization changed my entire approach to leadership. I started to see each interaction with my team as an opportunity to make their work life better, to help them grow, to show them what great leadership looks like.

A young front desk clerk named Alex stands out as a particularly powerful example of this. He was fresh out of college, and this was his first "real" job. I could have just seen him as another employee to train and manage. Instead, I saw an opportunity to shape his entire perception of what work could be.

I made sure to mentor Alex, to challenge him with new responsibilities, to celebrate his successes, and to turn his mistakes into learning opportunities. I wanted his first experience in the professional world to be positive and growth-oriented.

Years later, Alex reached out to me. He had become a successful hotel manager himself and was calling to thank me. "You were my first boss," he said, "and you showed me what good leadership looks like. I try to lead my team the same way you led us."

That conversation brought tears to my eyes. It drove home the profound impact we can have as leaders. We might not be someone's first boss, but we could be their first experience of great leadership—and that can shape their entire career.

But with this privilege comes great responsibility. The flip side is that poor leadership can be incredibly damaging. A bad boss can make someone dread coming to work, affect their mental health, and even make them question their career choice.

I've seen the effects of poor leadership firsthand. In one hotel I took over, morale was at rock bottom. The previous manager had been a micromanager who never trusted his staff to make decisions. He never made personal connections with staff, and when they did come to him, he always made it clear that he had other more important issues to attend to. The result was a team that felt disempowered, unmotivated, and unhappy.

It took months of consistent, positive leadership to turn that situation around. I had to show the team, day in and day out, that I trusted them, valued their input, and believed in their abilities. Slowly but surely, I saw the change. People started to take initiative, to smile more, to take pride in their work.

That experience reinforced for me the weight of the privilege we hold as leaders. Our actions, words, and attitudes extend far beyond what we might imagine.

This understanding of leadership as a privilege isn't just my personal philosophy. It's a perspective shared by some of the most respected leaders in the world. One story that always resonates with me is about Colin Powell, the former U.S. secretary of state and chairman of the Joint Chiefs of Staff.

During his time as secretary of state, Powell demonstrated a profound understanding of leadership through a simple yet powerful interaction. One day, he left his grand office and protective security detail to visit the Pentagon garage, where most of the workers worked for minimum wage. The attendants were surprised to see the secretary, initially thinking he was lost, and they offered to help him find his way back to his office.

Powell explained he just wanted to chat, and eventually asked them a question that had puzzled him: in their overcrowded garage where cars needed to be stacked behind one another, how did they decide which cars would be positioned for quick retrieval and which would be blocked in? Their response revealed a simple truth about leadership. Anyone who's endured the notorious DC traffic knows that garage positioning isn't just a minor convenience—it's practically a survival strategy! Getting that coveted front spot means the difference between making it home for dinner or spending another hour inching along the Beltway while your takeout gets cold. Their response to Powell's simple question would uncover an unexpected insight about organizational priorities and the subtle ways leadership decisions manifest in everyday operations.

With knowing smiles, one attendant explained their system: "Mr. Secretary, it goes like this: When you drive in, if you lower the window, look out, smile, or know our name, you're number one to get out. But if you look straight ahead, don't show you see us or that we are doing something for you, well, you are likely to be one of the last to get out."

Powell immediately recognized the leadership lesson and shared it with his senior staff: "You can never err by treating everyone in the building with respect, thoughtfulness, and a kind word." This story illustrates a crucial aspect of leadership privilege: the power to make people feel valued. Powell understood that his position gave him the ability to significantly impact how people felt about their work and their place in the organization.

Moreover, Powell's actions demonstrate another crucial aspect of leadership privilege: the ability to set the tone for the entire organization. By treating every employee with respect and dignity, regardless of their position, Powell was modeling the behavior he expected from others. He recognized that every person in an organization has value and wants that value to be acknowledged. As Powell himself noted, "Taking care of employees is perhaps the best form of kindness."[1]

This approach to leadership isn't just about being nice—it's about being effective. When people feel valued and respected, they're more engaged, more motivated, and more likely to go above and beyond in their work. By recognizing the privilege of his position and using it to uplift others, Powell was creating a more positive and productive work environment for everyone.

As leaders, we have the privilege of shaping not just the work, but the lives of the people we lead. We can choose to use that privilege to create positive, empowering environments where people can thrive. Or we can squander it, creating toxic environments that drain people's energy and enthusiasm.

So, how can we honor this privilege? Here are a few key principles I've learned:

1 **Lead with gratitude:** Never forget that your team chooses to show up every day. They could find another job, but they've chosen to be part of your team. Show appreciation for that choice.

2 **Invest in growth:** See it as your responsibility to help your team members grow, both professionally and personally. Provide opportunities for learning and development.

3 **Be the example:** Remember that your team is always watching. How you handle stress, how you treat others, how you

---

1 Colin Powell, "Kindness Works," *Parade,* May 20, 2012, https://parade.com/121472/colinlpowell/120520-colin-powell-kindness-works/

approach challenges—it all sets the tone for your entire organization.

4 **Listen and empathize:** Take the time to understand your team members' perspectives, challenges, and aspirations. Show them that their voices matter.

5 **Recognize every role:** Like Colin Powell, make an effort to acknowledge and appreciate every role in your organization. From the front-line workers to the behind-the-scenes support staff, every person contributes to your organization's success.

The privilege of leadership isn't something to take lightly. It's a gift that comes with the potential to positively impact numerous lives. Every day, we have the opportunity to make someone's work life better, to inspire growth, to show what great leadership looks like.

So the next time you walk into your workplace, take a moment to remember the privilege you hold. Look at each team member and think about the impact you can have on their life. Because at the end of the day, leadership isn't just about managing tasks or achieving goals. It's about touching lives, shaping careers, and creating an impact that extends far beyond the walls of your organization.

Embrace this privilege. Honor it. And use it to create a workplace where people don't just come to work, but come to thrive. It all starts with recognizing the value in every person. Your words, your actions, your attention—they all have the power to make a profound difference in someone's life. That's the true privilege of leadership.

Reflection Question: Think about your most impactful leader or mentor—how did they use their privilege of leadership to make a difference in your life, and how can you do the same for others?

CHAPTER 3

The No Bad Day Policy: Maintaining a Positive Presence

Early in my career, I had a manager—let's call him Tom—who taught me a valuable lesson about leadership, though not in the way he intended. Tom was brilliant at his job in many ways, but he had one major flaw: his mood was as unpredictable as the weather.

Every morning, the staff watched Tom walk through the doors with bated breath. Would today be a good day or a bad day? Would we be greeted with a smile or a scowl? The uncertainty created an intense tension that hung over the hotel.

On good days, Tom was charismatic and inspiring. He'd bounce around the hotel, cracking jokes and motivating the team. But on bad days—well, those were a different story. He'd snap at the slightest mistake, micromanage every detail, and generally make everyone feel on edge.

One week we were all stressed as we prepared for a major conference. On Monday, Tom was in a great mood, praising our hard work and boosting morale. By Wednesday, though, the pressure had gotten to him. He stormed through the hotel, criticizing everything from the way the napkins were folded to the tone of voice used at the front desk.

The impact on the team was immediate. Productivity plummeted. Mistakes increased. The positive energy that had been building earlier in the week evaporated. Even worse, this rollercoaster of emotions started to affect our guests. They could sense the tension, and it colored their experience at our hotel.

It was during this time that I made a promise to myself: if I ever became a leader, I would never subject my team to this kind of emotional whiplash. I realized that as a leader, you don't have the luxury of having a "bad day"—at least not in front of your team.

When I became a general manager, I implemented what I called the "No Bad Day Policy." And let me tell you, this is one of the few times you'll ever hear me use the word "policy"—I usually call it the "p word" because it's almost a dirty word to me. Too often, policies trap people into rigid thinking and prevent them from doing what's right for their guests and their team. I believe in being comfortable operating in the gray area, letting our values and judgment guide us rather than strict rules. But in this case, the No Bad Day Policy isn't really a policy at all—it's more of a mindset, a commitment to maintaining a positive presence for your team. This mindset doesn't mean pretending to be happy all the time or bottling up your emotions. It means understanding the weight of your presence as a leader and the impact your mood has on your entire team.

This approach to leadership is about being consistent, approachable, and supportive, regardless of what's going on behind the scenes. It means that if I'm having a challenging day, I take a moment to myself—step outside, take a few deep breaths, or even call a trusted friend or mentor for a quick pep talk.

The results were remarkable. Without the constant anxiety about the boss's mood, my teams were more relaxed, more productive, and more creative. They felt safe to bring up issues or ideas, knowing they wouldn't meet an unpredictable response.

Now, you might be wondering, "How can I maintain this positive presence consistently, especially when things get tough?" This question reminds me of the influence my friend Jon Gordon has had on my approach to leadership. In his transformative book *The Energy Bus,* Jon shares powerful principles about choosing to fuel your life and work with positive energy. Positivity is a choice we make each day, and that choice affects everyone around us.

In any organization, people either contribute to a positive atmosphere or detract from it. As leaders, we have a special responsibility in this regard. Our energy and attitude set the tone. When we choose positivity, it is contagious. When we let negativity take hold, that spreads just as quickly.

Let me give you an example from my experience. We were going through a particularly challenging period at one of my hotels. We were understaffed, our occupancy was down, and we were facing some tough financial decisions. It would have been easy to let the stress and negativity affect me and the entire team.

Instead, I decided to maintain a positive presence. Every morning, I gathered the team for a quick huddle. We started with a round of appreciation, where each person shared something they were grateful for or something a colleague had done well. Then, we focused on our wins, no matter how small. Maybe we'd received a great guest review, or someone had come up with a clever cost-saving idea. Finally, we set our intention for the day, focusing on what we could control and improve.

This daily practice didn't magically solve all our problems, but it did something powerful. It shifted our focus from what was going wrong to what was going right. It created a sense of team unity and purpose. And most importantly, it injected a dose of positive energy into our day right from the start.

I noticed that team members started adopting this positive attitude themselves. They became more solution-oriented, more supportive of each other, and more resilient in the face of challenges. Our morning huddles became a catalyst for positive change throughout the organization.

But here's the thing: as the leader, I had to be the chief ambassador of positivity. If I had shown up one day with a negative attitude, complaining about our challenges instead of focusing on solutions, it would have undermined everything we were trying to build. My commitment to maintaining a positive presence was crucial in sustaining our momentum.

Here are some strategies I've found helpful in maintaining a positive presence:

1 **Start your day right:** For me, this means blasting uplifting music during my drive to work. Sometimes my fellow drivers catch me dancing and singing in my car, but that energy carries me through the day. Find what works for you—whether it's meditation, exercise, reading something inspirational, or simply listing things you're grateful for. This sets a positive tone for your day.

2 **Choose your attitude:** Although you can't always control what happens to you, you can always control how you respond. Choose to approach challenges with optimism and a solution-oriented mindset.

3 **Practice gratitude:** Regularly express appreciation for your team members and celebrate wins, no matter how small. This creates a culture of positivity and recognition.

4 **Take care of yourself:** You can't pour from an empty cup. Make sure you're taking care of your own physical and mental health so you have the energy to support your team.

5 **Surround yourself with positive people:** Seek out colleagues and mentors who maintain an optimistic outlook. Their positive energy will help fuel your own.

6 **Address negativity promptly:** If you notice persistent negativity in your organization, address the issue quickly. Sometimes, a simple conversation about the impact of attitude can make a big difference.

7 **Be authentic:** Maintaining a positive presence doesn't mean being fake or ignoring real issues. It's about approaching all situations, even difficult ones, with a constructive, solution-focused attitude.

Let me share a story that illustrates the power of this approach. A few years ago, I was hired to take over a hotel that was struggling. Morale was low, customer complaints were high, and the staff seemed resigned to mediocrity. On my first day, I gathered the team and introduced the No Bad Day Policy.

At first, staff members were skeptical. I could see it in their eyes— they'd heard motivational speeches before, and nothing had changed. But I was committed. Every day, I made a point of greeting each staff member with enthusiasm, regardless of what challenges we were facing. I started each meeting by highlighting positive feedback from guests and celebrating small wins.

One day, about a month into this new approach, I overheard a conversation between two of our department heads. One was clearly having a rough day, dealing with staffing challenges and guest complaints. The other leader said something that stopped me in my tracks: "Come on, you know what Ryan always says—no bad days! Let's tackle this together and figure out a solution. We can turn this into a success story for our next leadership meeting."

In that moment, I knew the culture was shifting. The positive attitude was spreading, and it wasn't just coming from me anymore. The leadership team was embracing it and supporting each other in maintaining it.

Over the next six months, we saw remarkable changes. Customer satisfaction scores improved dramatically. Staff turnover, which had been a major problem, dropped to almost zero. Most importantly, there was a notable change in the atmosphere of the hotel. You could feel the positive energy the moment you walked through the doors.

But maintaining this positive presence isn't always easy. There will be days when you're tested, when it feels like everything is going wrong. I'll never forget when we experienced a power outage during a major conference at a hotel I was managing in Florida. It would have been easy to let stress and frustration show, to become discouraged and negative.

Instead, I gathered the team and said, "Alright, folks, this is our moment to shine. Yes, we have a challenge, but think about the story our guests will tell if we handle this with positivity and creativity. Let's show them what we're made of!" The team rose to the occasion magnificently, turning a potential disaster into a showcase of our problem-solving skills and positive attitude. Our front desk staff quickly transformed the lobby into an impromptu gathering space, setting up battery-powered lanterns and creating a warm, intimate atmosphere. The culinary team, led by our resourceful executive chef, salvaged the conference lunch by setting up a creative outdoor buffet with cold selections and grilled items prepared on our patio kitchen. Perhaps most touching was how our housekeeping team went floor by floor with flashlights, checking on guests and delivering bottled water and reassuring updates. When power was restored three hours later, we received countless compliments about how our team had made an unexpected disruption feel more like a unique adventure.

The No Bad Day Policy isn't about denying the existence of problems or pretending everything is perfect. It's about choosing how you respond to the challenges that inevitably arise. It's about being the kind of leader who inspires and energizes, rather than one who drains and discourages.

As you implement this approach, you'll likely find that it doesn't just transform your workplace—it transforms you. You'll discover reserves of resilience and positivity you didn't know you had. You'll find yourself better equipped to handle stress and challenges in all areas of your life.

And perhaps most importantly, you'll be creating a lasting impact on the people you lead. Years from now, your team members may not remember every conversation you had or every goal you achieved. But they will remember how you made them feel. They'll remember the leader who showed up every day with a positive attitude, who believed in them and inspired them to be their best selves.

That's the power of the No Bad Day Policy. That's the kind of leader I challenge you to be. When you commit to maintaining a positive presence, you're not just changing your workplace—you're changing lives. There's no greater privilege or responsibility in leadership than that.

Reflection Question: What specific strategies could you develop to maintain a positive presence during challenging times, and what triggers do you need to recognize in yourself to implement these strategies effectively?

CHAPTER 4

Lead with Your Heart:
The Kindness Advantage

Mr. Johnson, a challenging repeat guest I had as an assistant manager at a bustling downtown hotel, seemed to complain about everything. The city view he "specifically requested" was partially obscured by an adjacent building, the water pressure in his shower was "completely inadequate," and the breakfast buffet's yogurt wasn't his preferred brand. You name it, he had a problem with it.

One morning, I was working the front desk when Mr. Johnson stormed up, his face red with anger. "This is the worst hotel I've ever stayed in!" he shouted, loud enough for everyone in the lobby to hear. "I demand to speak to the manager right now!"

I took a deep breath, preparing myself for the confrontation. But before I could respond, our general manager, Christine, appeared as if from nowhere. What happened next was a textbook example of leadership.

Christine didn't get defensive. She didn't argue. Instead, she smiled warmly and said, "Mr. Johnson, I'm so sorry to hear you're not enjoying your stay. Please, let's sit down and talk about it. I want to hear everything."

For the next thirty minutes, Christine sat with Mr. Johnson in the lobby lounge. She listened intently, nodding and taking notes. She asked questions, showing genuine concern for his experience. By the end of the conversation, Mr. Johnson's anger had completely dissipated. In fact, he was smiling and thanking Christine for her time.

Later, I asked Christine how she managed to turn the situation around so completely. Her answer was simple: "I led with my heart. Kindness isn't weakness, Ryan. It's the most powerful tool we have."

What I didn't fully appreciate at the time was Christine's subtle but strategic decision to move Mr. Johnson away from the front desk to the quiet lobby lounge. She later shared with me one of her most valuable leadership principles: when handling any confrontation, whether with a customer or team member, the first step is often changing the environment. "People naturally perform for an audience," she explained. "Remove the audience, and you remove the performance. In a more private setting, you're usually dealing with the real person and the real issue." This simple yet powerful approach has transformed countless heated situations into productive conversations throughout my career.

Leading with kindness and empathy isn't just about being nice—it's a strategic advantage. When we approach leadership with compassion, we create an environment where people feel heard, valued, and motivated to do their best.

Now, I know what you might be thinking: "Ryan, this all sounds great, but in the real world, don't we sometimes need to be tough to get results?" It's a fair question, and one I often get.

That's when I share one of my key leadership principles, one that always gets a laugh: "Don't be a jackass."

Yes, you heard that right. "Don't be a jackass" is a fundamental principle of positive leadership. Now, I know it might sound a bit crude, but hear me out.

You see, too often in the business world, we encounter leaders who believe that being tough, harsh, or even mean is the way to get results. They yell, they criticize, they rule by fear. But here's the thing—that approach doesn't work. At least, not in the long run.

When I share this principle, I can always see the recognition in people's eyes. We've all encountered that boss, that colleague, that person in a position of power who thinks being a jackass is the way to lead. And we all know how it feels to be on the receiving end of that kind of leadership—it's demotivating, demoralizing, and, ultimately, counterproductive.

People respond far more positively to kindness, understanding, and positive leadership than they do to negativity. When you lead with kindness—when you choose not to be a jackass—you create an environment where people want to do their best work. They're not just working to avoid criticism or punishment; they're working because they feel valued, respected, and motivated.

I worked with a manager who we'll call Bob early in my career. Bob was the epitome of the "jackass" leader. He yelled at staff in front of customers, criticized every little mistake, and generally created an atmosphere of fear and anxiety. The result? High turnover, low morale, and a team that was too afraid to take initiative or go the extra mile.

Contrast that with Christine. Christine led with kindness and understanding. She addressed issues privately and constructively, celebrated successes publicly, and always made her team feel supported.

The difference was night and day. Under Christine's leadership, the team was more innovative, more customer-focused, and enjoyed coming to work.

So, when I say, "Don't be a jackass," what I'm really saying is to choose kindness. Choose understanding. Choose to be the type of leader people want to follow, not because they have to but because they want to.

This doesn't mean being a pushover or ignoring problems. It means addressing issues with empathy and respect. It means setting high standards while providing the support and resources your team needs to meet those standards. It means creating an environment where people feel safe to take risks, to innovate, and to grow. It means recognizing that your employees are human beings with lives, feelings, and challenges outside of work.

I've applied this lesson countless times. When I took over struggling hotels, my first step was always to listen—really listen—to the staff. What were their frustrations? What did they need to do their jobs better? By showing that I genuinely cared about their experiences and well-being, I was able to build trust and motivate teams to achieve remarkable turnarounds.

But leading with your heart isn't just about how you handle crises or complaints. It's about the small, everyday interactions too. It's about remembering an employee's birthday, or asking about their sick parent. It's about celebrating their successes and supporting them through their challenges.

I once had an employee who was struggling with her performance. The easy path would have been to put her on a performance improvement plan or even let her go. Instead, I sat down with her and simply asked, "How can I help?" It turned out she was dealing with some personal issues that were affecting her work. By showing compassion and offering support, I was able to work with her to find a solution. Within a few months, she was one of our top performers.

When you lead with kindness, you create a culture where people feel safe to take risks, to innovate, and to give their all. You build loyalty that goes beyond a paycheck. You inspire your team to treat each other—and your customers—with the same level of compassion and care.

So, the next time you're faced with a challenging situation or a difficult conversation, think about Mr. Johnson and Christine. Take a deep breath, open your heart, and lead with kindness. And most importantly: don't be a jackass. You might be surprised at the results.

Positive leaders win. They win the respect of their team, the loyalty of their customers, and the success that comes from creating an environment where everyone can thrive. And it all starts with the simple decision to lead with your heart.

Reflection Question: Recall a time when someone showed you unexpected kindness in a professional setting. How did it affect you, and how can you create more of these moments for your team?

CHAPTER 5

Work-Life Harmony: Valuing Your Team's Personal Lives

One of the most important documents that I've developed over my career (and I share a copy of in my first book, *Thanks for Coming In Today*) is what I call my "expectations document." It's a list I would share with my management teams that outlines not just what I expected from them, but what they could expect from me as a leader. And one of the key points on that list always raised a few eyebrows: "I am not impressed when people turn a forty-hour work week into seventy."

In corporate America, there's often an unspoken expectation that working longer hours equals greater dedication or productivity. But in my experience, that's simply not true. In fact, I've found that people are generally better at their jobs when they have time to rest, recharge, and enjoy life outside of work.

I learned this lesson the hard way early in my career. I was working seventy- to eighty-hour weeks, thinking I was proving my worth and climbing the corporate ladder. But in reality, I was burning out. My work was suffering, my personal relationships were strained, and I was miserable. It was then that I realized: we work to live, not live to work.

When I became a leader, I made it my mission to create a culture that valued work-life balance—or, as Jeff Bezos, founder of Amazon, calls it, work-life harmony. Balance implies that work and life are opposing forces, when in reality, they should complement each other. Like instruments in an orchestra, when work and personal life are in harmony, they create something more meaningful than the sum of their parts.

I witnessed a powerful example of this work-life harmony when I was invited to keynote the Lee's Famous Recipe Chicken Restaurants' annual franchise conference. What struck me immediately was that they don't call it a conference—they call it their "family reunion."

When I asked CEO Ryan Weaver about why they use this terminology, his response struck me. "We call it a family reunion because that's exactly what it is," he explained. "These aren't just our franchisees—they're our family. When we get together, it's not just about business metrics and operations reviews. It's about celebrating our shared successes, supporting each other through challenges, and strengthening the bonds that make us who we are."

This wasn't just corporate speak—you could feel the difference in the atmosphere of their gathering. Unlike many corporate conferences, there was a genuine understanding that everyone had lives beyond their roles. People were sharing more than best practices; they were sharing life updates, family photos, and personal achievements. They had created something remarkable: a work environment where personal lives weren't separate from work lives—they were beautifully intertwined.

Being intentional about how and when you show up for your team is crucial to creating this work-life harmony. My lifelong friend Michael

Sucher, a proprietor for Outback Steakhouse, offers a perfect example of this principle in action. Every day, Michael spends the first fifteen minutes walking around his restaurant, greeting each employee, asking how they're doing, and listening closely to their responses.

"Look, if we want real hospitality in our restaurants," Michael says, "We've got to walk the walk ourselves. It's pretty simple—when our team feels taken care of, from their first interview all the way through their daily work, that's exactly how they'll treat each other and our guests."

Michael's insight gets to the heart of something I've observed throughout my career: the way we treat our employees directly mirrors how they'll treat our guests. When we make time to show genuine care and interest in our team members' lives, when we prioritize these daily interactions, we're not just being good leaders—we're modeling the very behaviors we want to see in our customer interactions.

The results speak for themselves in Michael's restaurants. That same warmth and hospitality he shows his team translates directly into the guest experience. His employees, feeling valued and seen, naturally extend that same consideration to their guests. It's a powerful reminder that hospitality isn't just a service strategy—it's a culture that starts with how we treat our own people.

This intentional approach to leadership requires discipline. It means blocking out time in your schedule specifically for these interactions. It means arriving early enough to have these conversations before the day gets hectic. Most importantly, it means being fully present in these moments—not checking your phone, not thinking about your next meeting, but engaging with each team member as a person. When we make this kind of time for our teams, it demonstrates that we value their well-being and understand they have lives beyond work.

One story that really drives this home for me involves a long-term employee at one of the hotels I managed. Mary had been with the company for over a decade and was one of our most dedicated team members. One day, while reviewing vacation schedules, I noticed that Mary had accrued over a month of unused vacation time.

When I asked her about it, Mary sheepishly admitted that she felt she couldn't take time off. "There's always so much to do," she said. "And none of the previous managers ever made me feel like it was okay to take a break."

I was stunned. Here was one of our best and most loyal employees, slowly burning out because she didn't feel empowered to use her well-earned time off. Right then and there, I told Mary that not only could she take her vacation time, but I was insisting on it. We sat down together and planned out how to use her accrued time over the next few months.

When Mary returned from her first two-week vacation in years, the change was remarkable. She was refreshed, energized, and full of new ideas. Her productivity soared, and her positive energy spread throughout the team.

From that point on, I made it a priority to actively encourage my team to use their vacation time. I regularly checked in with team members about their time-off plans. If someone hadn't taken a vacation in a while, I gently nudged them to do so.

But it's not just about vacation time. It's about creating a culture that respects people's lives outside of work. This means being flexible with schedules when possible, understanding when personal issues arise, and never expecting employees to be "always on."

I once had a team member who was struggling to balance work with caring for an elderly parent. Instead of penalizing her for needing a more flexible schedule, we worked together to find a solution that allowed her to meet her family obligations without sacrificing her work responsibilities. The result? A grateful, loyal employee who went above and beyond in her role.

It's important to remember that your employees are whole people with lives, families, hobbies, and responsibilities outside of work. When you respect and support that, you create a more engaged, more loyal, and ultimately more productive team.

So, make it known that you value your team's personal time. Encourage them to take their vacations. Be understanding when life happens. And most importantly, model this behavior yourself. Take your own vacation time, maintain reasonable work hours, and show your team that it's not just okay but essential to have a life outside of work.

By fostering a culture of work-life harmony, you'll build a team that's not just more productive, but happier, healthier, and more committed to your organization's success. After all, we're in the business of hospitality—and that should extend to how we treat our own people, too.

Reflection Question: How do your actions as a leader either support or hinder your team's work-life harmony, and what specific changes could you make to better support their well-being?

CHAPTER 6

Leading Through Crisis: Maintaining Positivity in Challenging Times

I've faced numerous challenges as a hotel leader–budget shortfalls, natural disasters, difficult owners. But nothing could have prepared me for the morning I had to gather my team in Florida and tell them they were being laid off due to the COVID-19 pandemic. No management book or leadership seminar can equip you for looking into the eyes of people who have given decades of their lives to our properties and telling them they no longer have jobs.

I was especially heartbroken to let go an executive housekeeper who had been with us for twenty-three years. She attended her team members' weddings and hosted baby showers. At work, she'd led her team to multiple wins and kept them upbeat during devastating hurricanes. When I regretfully told her she was being laid off, she hugged me and said, "It's okay, Ryan. This isn't your fault." Here I was, delivering the worst news of her professional life, and she was trying to comfort me. That moment crystallized for me both the challenge and the opportunity of leading through crisis—how do we maintain our humanity and positivity when everything around us seems to be falling apart?

The early days of the pandemic tested every leadership principle I'd ever learned or taught. It's one thing to talk about maintaining a positive presence when you're dealing with normal business challenges. It's quite another when you're facing a global crisis that's reshaping your entire industry.

After the pandemic, I spoke with a home healthcare system's leadership team. A nursing director approached me afterward with tears in her eyes. She shared how her team had faced similar burnout during COVID—not from layoffs, but from being overwhelmed and understaffed. As I listened to her story, it reinforced something I often tell my consulting clients: crisis leadership isn't just about managing the immediate challenge. It's about preserving your team's humanity and spirit through the darkest times. Her nurses, like my hotel staff, weren't just dealing with professional challenges—they were facing profound personal ones as well. This conversation reminded me that while industries may differ, the principles of positive leadership during crisis remain the same.

In fact, the principles of positive leadership become even more crucial during times of crisis. They're not just nice-to-have philosophies for good times—they're essential tools for surviving and eventually thriving through the toughest challenges.

In Florida, we faced a unique situation. While much of the country's hospitality industry remained shut down or heavily restricted, our properties quickly reopened (many never closed) with high occupancy rates. This might sound like good news, but it created its own set of overwhelming challenges.

Picture this: we were running near-full hotels with skeleton crews, a direct result of ownership's defensive response to pandemic uncertainties. As travel demand fluctuated unpredictably, many properties had cut staffing to bare minimums, fearing the business impact of this unprecedented crisis. The reality on the ground was stark—our remaining team members were shouldering the workload of two or three positions, stretching themselves thin to maintain service standards. They were not only physically exhausted but also grappling with genuine fears about their own health and safety. Adding to this pressure, they often faced increasingly hostile guests who, understanding little of our behind-the-scenes challenges, expressed their frustration with longer wait times and reduced services. This perfect storm of reduced staff, increased workload, and heightened guest expectations tested our team's resilience like never before.

I remember one particularly difficult day when one of our front desk agents, Nicole, came to my office in tears. A guest had screamed at her about having to wait for his room, calling her "lazy" and "incompetent." What the guest didn't know was that Nicole had been working twelve-hour shifts for the past week, doing everything from checking in guests to helping strip rooms because we were so short-staffed.

In that moment, I realized that maintaining positivity during crisis isn't about pretending everything is fine. It's about acknowledging the reality of the situation while still finding ways to support and uplift your team. I sat with Nicole, letting her express her frustration and validating her feelings. Then, together, we developed strategies for handling similar situations in the future. I assured her that she had my full support to step away when guests became abusive, and I would personally handle those interactions. More importantly, I shared specific examples of the extraordinary impact she'd had on other guests that week—the family she'd helped find a late-night pharmacy, the elderly couple she'd assisted with their luggage despite being swamped with check-ins. By the end of our conversation, Nicole was feeling better, reconnected to her purpose and value within our team. Sometimes, true leadership isn't about solving every problem, but about helping your team find their strength in the midst of challenges.

Here are some key lessons I learned about crisis leadership during this challenging period:

1 Balance Honesty with Compassion

Positive leadership doesn't mean sugarcoating difficult realities. When delivering challenging news to your team, be direct about the situation while showing genuine appreciation for their contributions. Your team needs both truth and support to maintain trust and motivation during difficult times.

2 Create Islands of Certainty

In times of crisis, people crave stability. Create what I call "islands of certainty"—predictable aspects of work life that your team can count on. This might mean maintaining consistent meeting schedules, preserving recognition programs, or establishing reliable communication channels. These touchpoints become anchors of normalcy when everything else feels unstable.

3 Protect Your People

Strengthen your commitment to protecting your team during high-pressure situations. Make it clear that while customer service excellence remains a priority, it never comes at the cost of your team's well-being. Empower your staff to step away from hostile situations, and be ready to personally intervene when needed. Your visible support in these moments builds lasting loyalty and trust.

4 Lead with Vulnerability

Show your team that authentic leadership includes acknowledging your own challenges. When you share your concerns while maintaining a sense of direction, you create genuine connections that strengthen team bonds. This balanced transparency helps create a culture of trust and mutual support.

5 Focus on Controllable Actions

Help your team channel their energy toward what they can influence rather than what they can't. Focus discussions on actionable steps: improving internal processes, strengthening team support systems, or enhancing service delivery within current constraints.

6 Maintain a Future Focus

Remind your team that challenges are temporary while building toward lasting solutions. Engage them in conversations about future improvements, growth opportunities, and how current challenges can lead to stronger operations. This forward-looking perspective helps maintain motivation and purpose during difficult periods.

7 Build Resilient Systems

Use challenging times to strengthen your operational foundation. Review and enhance your support systems, communication channels, and team development programs. Creating robust frameworks during difficult periods ensures your team emerges stronger and better prepared for future challenges.

Perhaps the most important lesson about leading through crisis: your team will mirror your attitude and approach. If you maintain hope while acknowledging challenges, balance realism with optimism, and continue to celebrate small wins while dealing with big problems, your team will follow suit.

I'm proud to say that many of our laid-off team members eventually returned when business recovered. Many told me they came back not just because they needed jobs, but because of how we handled the crisis—with transparency, compassion, and commitment to our people.

The pandemic taught me that positive leadership isn't just about managing success—it's about navigating through storms while keeping your humanity intact. It's about finding light in the darkness and helping others see it too. It's about maintaining hope without denying reality.

As leaders, we can't always control the crises that come our way, but we can control how we lead through them. By staying true to our principles of positive leadership, even in the most challenging times, we not only help our teams survive, we help them emerge stronger and more united than ever before.

In times of crisis, your team doesn't expect you to have all the answers. They just need to know that you're in it with them, that you care about them as people, and that you're committed to finding a way forward together. That's what positive leadership in crisis looks like. That's how we maintain our humanity when everything around us feels chaotic. And ultimately, that's how we emerge from crises not just intact, but stronger than before.

Reflection Question: Think about a recent crisis in your organization. How did your leadership actions help or hinder your team's ability to navigate it, and what would you do differently next time?

CHAPTER 7

Positive Change Management: Leading Teams Through Transformation

Sometimes being positive means making tough decisions. When I was brought in to turn around struggling operations, I often encountered a situation that many leaders are hesitant to address: the presence of poor leaders who were poisoning the workplace culture. In these situations, I've learned that direct, honest conversations are essential—and sometimes, the most positive action for the team is to part ways with those who undermine the culture we're building. While these decisions aren't easy, they're necessary to create the healthy, thriving environment our team members deserve.

The metrics told one story at a struggling property I was charged with turning around in Florida—low guest satisfaction scores, declining revenue, high turnover. But the real story was written on the faces of the employees. You could feel the tension, see the defeated looks, and sense the resignation that "this is just how things are."

After a few days of observation and conversations with staff, the source became clear. Two of the department heads had created what I call "kingdoms of fear" within their areas. They ruled through intimidation, played favorites, and undermined any attempts at positive change by other leaders. While they had impressive resumes and years of experience, they were what I've come to recognize as threats to the positive mission.

Here's the thing about poor leaders: keeping them isn't just bad for morale—it actively undermines your own leadership credibility. Your team watches everything you do, and when they see you tolerating toxic leadership, they start to question your commitment to creating a positive workplace. They wonder, "If they really care about us, why do they let this continue?"

I've had many conversations with other executives who hesitate to remove problematic leaders, usually citing reasons like, "But they've been here for years," or "They know the operation inside and out," or simply just fear of the position being open. What these executives don't realize is that by trying to avoid short-term pain, they're allowing long-term damage to fester.

In that Florida hotel, I made the difficult but necessary decision to replace those department heads within my first month. The immediate response from the team was telling. One housekeeper, who'd been with the property for over a decade, came to my office with tears in her eyes. "Thank you," she said. "We'd almost lost hope that things could be different."

But removing negative leaders is just the first step in managing positive change. The real work comes in rebuilding trust, restoring confidence, and creating a new vision for the future. This became intensely clear during an unprecedented natural disaster that struck one of our properties.

When a hurricane devastated a significant portion of a beachfront hotel I was overseeing, we found ourselves navigating changes that none of us could have imagined. We weren't just dealing with typical operational changes—we were facing fundamental transformations in how we did business, often with immediate safety implications. The uncertainty was overwhelming for everyone as we dealt with structural damage, displaced staff, and concerned guests.

Managing change positively during crisis requires what I call the "Three Cs": clarity, consistency, and care.

In this situation, clarity meant being honest about what we knew and what we didn't know. When we had to close certain areas of the property and implement emergency protocols, we didn't just announce changes—we explained the reasoning behind them to both guests and employees. When we weren't sure about restoration timelines, we admitted it while sharing our plans for different scenarios.

Consistency came through maintaining our positive leadership practices even as parts of our property lay in ruins. We kept our daily huddles (though in temporary locations), continued our recognition programs, and stayed committed to our core values. This gave our team anchor points during uncertain times.

Care meant showing genuine concern for our team's physical and emotional well-being. We created support systems for employees who lost their homes, adjusted schedules to accommodate personal recovery efforts, and made sure our team knew that their safety and stability were our top priority.

But perhaps the most important lesson I've learned about managing change positively is this: change isn't something you do to your team—it's something you do with them. When people feel like participants rather than victims of change, their entire perspective shifts.

I saw this in action when we needed to completely reimagine our guest service protocols during the recovery period. Instead of simply dictating new procedures, we involved our front-line staff in developing solutions. Their insights were invaluable, and their buy-in was automatic because they had helped create the changes.

This collaborative approach to change management doesn't mean you need consensus on every decision. Sometimes, as with removing toxic leaders, you need to make tough calls unilaterally. But it does mean creating an environment where people feel heard and valued throughout the change process.

Building resilience through change requires "positive preparation." This means:

1   Creating a strong foundation of trust before major changes are needed

2   Maintaining transparent communication throughout the change process

3   Celebrating small wins along the way

4   Supporting team members who struggle with the changes

5   Acknowledging and learning from setbacks

6   Keeping the focus on the positive vision of the future

Your team's reaction to change often mirrors your own attitude toward it. If you approach change with fear and anxiety, that's what your team will feel. But if you can maintain a positive, forward-looking perspective while acknowledging the challenges, you create an environment where change becomes an opportunity rather than a threat.

During the hurricane recovery, I saw our teams adapt and innovate in remarkable ways. For instance, our restaurant crew transformed our parking lot into an emergency food distribution center, serving hot meals to first responders and displaced families. They didn't just survive the devastation—they found ways to thrive despite it. The key was having leaders who could maintain positivity without denying reality, who could acknowledge challenges while inspiring hope.

Managing change positively doesn't mean pretending everything is fine when it isn't. It means facing challenges honestly while maintaining faith in your team's ability to overcome them. It means making tough decisions when necessary while always keeping your positive mission in focus. And sometimes, it means being strong enough to remove the obstacles—including toxic leaders—that stand in the way of positive transformation.

Change is constant in business today. Successful organizations don't resist change; they learn to manage it positively. By building a foundation of trust, maintaining clear communication, and showing genuine care for your team, you can turn periods of change from times of fear into opportunities for growth.

Your role as a positive leader isn't to shield your team from change, but to guide them through it with clarity, consistency, and care. When you do this effectively, you don't just manage change—you transform your organization in ways that last long after the immediate changes are complete.

Reflection Question: Think about a significant change you're currently managing or anticipating. How can you apply the principles of positive change management to make this transition more successful for your team?

CHAPTER 8

Above and Beyond: Exceptional Service in Challenging Situations

It's easy to provide good service when everything's going smoothly. The true test of a team's spirit—and a leader's impact—comes when things get tough. This story from Wisconsin stands as a perfect example of how exceptional service shines brightest during challenging moments.

I was heading to speak at an association's annual meeting in central Wisconsin. Now, for a Florida guy like me, traveling to the middle of Wisconsin in winter was already an adventure. But little did I know, the real adventure was just beginning.

My flight was delayed, connections were missed, and by the time I finally landed at the small Central Wisconsin Airport, it was well after midnight. Exhausted and a bit frazzled, I walked out of the airport, ready to catch an Uber to my hotel, which was over an hour away.

That's when I hit my first snag. There was no Uber. In fact, there were no ride-sharing services available at all. I stood there, luggage in hand, wondering how on earth I was going to get to my hotel in the middle of the night in a town I'd never been to before.

Slightly panicked, I made my way to the rental car counters. The first two were completely out of cars. My heart sank. The third and final counter belonged to Avis, and as I approached, I was already preparing myself for disappointment.

But that's when I met Levi.

Levi was a young woman working the late-night shift at the Avis counter. As I walked up, visibly stressed and travel-worn, she looked at me with the brightest smile I'd ever seen and said, "Don't worry, I have cars!"

Those five words, delivered with such genuine warmth and enthusiasm, immediately lifted a weight off my shoulders. But Levi wasn't done yet. As she processed my rental, she chatted with me like we were old friends, asking about my trip, why I was in Wisconsin, and if I needed any recommendations for my stay.

Her positivity was infectious. Despite the late hour and the stressful journey, I found myself smiling and relaxing. When everything was sorted, I couldn't help but ask her, "Levi, are you always this happy at work?"

Her response stuck with me: "Yes, because I love my boss!"

In that moment, I was reminded of one of the most fundamental truths of leadership: people join companies, but they stay—or leave—because of their bosses.

Levi's exceptional service wasn't just about her individual personality (though that certainly played a part). It was a reflection of the positive work environment her boss had created. Her leader had fostered a culture where employees felt valued and motivated to go above and beyond, even in challenging situations.

Think about it. Levi was working a late-night shift at a small airport rental car counter. It would have been easy for her to be grumpy, to do the bare minimum, to count the minutes until she could go home. But instead, she was a beacon of positivity, turning what could have been a terrible experience for a weary traveler into a memorable one for all the right reasons.

I was so moved by Levi's exceptional service that I actually reached out to Avis to share the story of her impact that night. While I wish I could say this always happens—that great service always gets recognized—the truth is, most of the time it doesn't. Leaders often don't get to hear about how their positive influence extends out through their team members to touch others' lives. But that's what makes positive leadership so powerful: by creating an environment where people like Levi feel appreciated and motivated, leaders set in motion countless positive interactions that extend far beyond their immediate team, whether they ever hear about them or not.

As leaders, we need to be mindful that our influence extends beyond our direct interactions with our team. The way we lead, the culture we create, it all trickles down to how our team interacts with customers, especially in challenging situations.

So, how can we create a culture where exceptional service becomes the norm, even when things get tough? Here are a few strategies I've found effective:

1 **Lead by example:** Show your team what going above and beyond looks like. When they see you putting in extra effort, it inspires them to do the same.

2 **Celebrate exceptional service:** When team members go out of their way to help a customer, make sure it's recognized and celebrated. This reinforces the behavior and shows others what's valued in your organization.

3   **Empower your team:** Give your employees the authority to make decisions that benefit the customer. When they don't have to run every little thing by a manager, they can respond more quickly and effectively to customer needs.

4   **Provide the right tools and training:** Make sure your team has what they need to provide exceptional service. This includes both tangible tools and the knowledge to handle difficult situations.

5   **Encourage problem-solving:** Teach your team to look for solutions, not just identify problems. This mindset is crucial for handling challenging situations effectively.

Exceptional service isn't about never having problems. It's about how you and your team respond when problems arise. It's about turning potential negative experiences into positive ones.

Levi could have simply rented me a car and sent me on my way. Instead, she turned a stressful situation into a positive memory—one that I'm still sharing years later. And she did it because her leader had created an environment where that level of service was the norm, not the exception.

As leaders, our challenge is to create a culture where the Levis of our organization can shine. Where going above and beyond isn't extraordinary—it's just how we do things. When we do that, we're improving customer service but also creating experiences, building loyalty, and setting our businesses apart in a crowded marketplace.

So, the next time you're faced with a challenging situation, remember Levi. Remember that smile, that enthusiasm, that willingness to go above and beyond. And ask yourself: Am I creating the kind of environment where my team can rise to that level? Am I empowering my Levis to shine?

That's what positive leadership is all about. It's about creating a chain reaction of positivity that extends from you to your team, to your customers, and beyond. And it all starts with you.

Reflection Question: What barriers currently exist in your organization that prevent team members from delivering exceptional service, and how can you remove them to empower your team?

CHAPTER 9

Recognition: Celebrating Work Wins and Life Milestones

One of my favorite leadership habits started with a simple stop at Starbucks. I was picking up my morning coffee when I had an idea: what if I could give team members an immediate "thank you" when I caught them doing something extraordinary? That day, I bought a stack of five-dollar Starbucks gift cards and started carrying them in my pocket. It turned out to be one of the best leadership investments I've ever made.

Shortly after buying the gift cards, I was walking through our lobby when I saw Kimi, one of our front desk agents, going above and beyond for a frustrated guest. The guest had lost his phone somewhere in the hotel, and Kimi didn't just take down his information—she personally retraced his steps with him, calling the phone repeatedly until they found it wedged between chairs in the restaurant. The look of relief on the guest's face was matched only by Kimi's triumphant smile.

As the guest walked away (checking his text messages) I approached

Kimi. "That was exceptional service," I said, handing her a Starbucks card. The surprise and appreciation on her face was wonderful, but what happened next was even better.

Word spread quickly about the Starbucks cards. Soon, team members weren't just doing great work hoping to get a card—they were excitedly telling me about their colleagues' exceptional service moments. "Ryan, did you see what Joel did in valet today?" or "You should have seen how Carlos handled that difficult situation in the restaurant!"

It wasn't about the monetary value of the cards—five dollars won't change anyone's life. It was about the immediate recognition, the fact that their leader was paying attention and appreciating their efforts in the moment. That small gesture created a culture where everyone started looking for and celebrating wins, both big and small.

But understanding the power of recognition wasn't just something I learned as a leader—I experienced it firsthand as an employee. I'll never forget when I was expecting my son, Charlie. I was working for a large hotel chain at the time, and while I had a good professional relationship with my senior executive, Michael, I wouldn't say we were close.

So you can imagine my surprise when, a few days after Charlie was born, a package arrived at my home. Inside was a beautiful, personalized baby blanket, along with a heartfelt note from Michael congratulating me on becoming a father.

I was touched. This wasn't a corporate gift or a perfunctory gesture. Michael had taken the time to choose something personal and meaningful. That blanket became one of Charlie's favorites, and every time I saw it, I was reminded of the power of personal recognition. It strengthened my loyalty to the company and my respect for Michael as a leader. I felt valued not just for my work, but as a person.

The most meaningful recognition isn't about the monetary value—it's about showing people that you see them, you value them, and you care about what's happening in their lives.

Recognition isn't just about rewarding good service or celebrating business wins. It's about acknowledging both professional achievements and personal milestones. When we recognize the whole person—not just the employee—we create deeper connections and stronger teams.

In our daily huddles, we made it a point to recognize both kinds of achievements. One morning at a property I managed in St. Louis stands out in my memory. Ashley, our front desk agent, spoke up during our recognition time. "I want to recognize Jorge from our bell team," she said. "Yesterday, during that awful snowstorm, I saw him out in the parking lot helping a guest scrape snow off their car. The guest hadn't even asked—Jorge just saw them struggling through the lobby windows and grabbed a scraper. That's the kind of above-and-beyond service that makes us special."

That public recognition did two important things: it celebrated Jorge's initiative, and it showed everyone else the kind of actions we value. Within weeks, I noticed other team members looking for similar opportunities to help guests proactively.

We also created a "Caught in the Act" program where anyone could drop a note when they caught a colleague going above and beyond. Each week, we'd read these notes aloud during our team meeting. It was a way to ensure that no good deed, no matter how small, went unnoticed.

But perhaps even more important than celebrating professional wins is honoring personal milestones. Work is just one part of our team members' lives, and when we acknowledge their personal achievements and life events, we show that we care about them as people, not just employees.

I'll never forget the day Mario, one of our line cooks, achieved his U.S. citizenship. We turned the employee cafeteria into a celebration space, complete with American flags and a cake decorated like the stars and stripes. The entire team gathered to congratulate him, and watching Mario beam with pride as he showed everyone his citizenship certificate reminded me why these celebrations matter so much. This wasn't just a personal achievement for Mario—it was a moment that brought our entire team closer together.

These celebrations, whether for professional wins or personal milestones, had an impact on our team morale and performance. Employee satisfaction scores went up. Turnover went down. And our guest satisfaction scores improved dramatically. But perhaps the most significant change was in the overall atmosphere of the hotel. There was a real sense of family, of belonging.

I made it a priority to keep track of important dates and milestones. Birthdays, work anniversaries, graduations—these were all opportunities to show our team that we cared about them as individuals, not just as employees. We'd celebrate when someone bought their first home, got married, or welcomed a new baby. These weren't just personal events—they were moments that strengthened our entire team.

But here's the key: celebration isn't just about the big moments. It's about creating a culture where recognition and appreciation are part of everyday life. This means the following:

1   **Making recognition immediate and specific:** Like those Starbucks cards in my pocket, don't wait to celebrate good work.

2   **Encouraging peer-to-peer recognition:** Some of the most meaningful recognition comes from colleagues because they intimately understand the daily challenges and unsung

moments of excellence in ways managers cannot. These acknowledgments carry special weight precisely because they come from someone who has walked in those same shoes and knows exactly what it takes to excel in that role.

3 **Celebrating both professional and personal achievements:** Show that you care about the whole person.

4 **Making celebrations inclusive:** Find ways to involve the entire team in recognitions and celebrations.

5 **Being consistent:** Don't let busy times or challenges prevent you from taking time to celebrate.

6 **Getting creative with recognition:** Sometimes the most memorable celebrations are the unexpected ones.

7 **Making it personal:** Generic recognition feels hollow—take the time to make it specific and meaningful.

Creating this culture of celebration doesn't happen overnight. It requires commitment and consistency from leadership. But the returns are immeasurable. When people feel valued and appreciated—both for their work and for who they are as individuals—they bring their best selves to work every day.

I've seen this play out countless times throughout my career. Teams that celebrate together stay together. They work harder for each other, support each other through challenges, and create better experiences for guests.

One of my favorite traditions was our monthly luncheons where we'd recognize all sorts of achievements. We'd celebrate the front desk agent who got a guest review mentioning them by name, the housekeeper who found and returned a valuable item to a guest, the maintenance worker who fixed a problem before it became a guest issue.

These celebrations did more than just recognize achievements—they helped us know each other better as people. They created connections that went beyond job titles and departments. They made us stronger as a team.

This impact of recognition on organizational excellence isn't limited to hospitality. I've seen it validated across industries, including in my work with Old Dominion Freight Line (ODFL). The company's remarkable achievement of winning the MASTIO Quality Award for fifteen consecutive years (and running at the time this book was published) speaks volumes about its commitment to consistent excellence. When I asked Chip Overbey, a senior vice president at ODFL, about the role of positive leadership in maintaining such high standards, his response reinforced everything I've learned about the power of recognition.

"Our success is built on creating an environment where people feel valued," Chip explained. This philosophy has earned ODFL recognition as one of Forbes' Best Large Employers, but more importantly, it's created a culture where team members are motivated to deliver exceptional service day after day. It's a powerful reminder that when organizations prioritize recognizing and valuing their people, the results naturally follow.

This principle holds true whether you're managing a hotel, running a freight company, or leading any other type of organization. When people feel valued, they consistently perform at their best. It's why at ODFL, as in the most successful hotels I've managed, recognition isn't just a program—it's woven into the fabric of daily operations.

As a leader, you set the tone for celebration in your organization. Your team will follow your lead. If you make recognition and celebration a priority, they will too. If you take the time to acknowledge both professional and personal milestones, you create an environment where people feel valued for who they are, not just what they do.

So keep those Starbucks cards in your pocket. Keep track of birthdays and anniversaries. Celebrate the big wins and the small ones. When you create a culture of celebration, you're not just building a better workplace—you're building a community where people can thrive, grow, and achieve their full potential.

And isn't that what great leadership is all about?

Reflection Question: How do you currently celebrate your team's achievements, both big and small, and what new recognition practices could you implement to make people feel more valued?

CHAPTER 10

Roll Up Your Sleeves: The Power of Present Leadership

One of the most powerful tools in a leader's arsenal isn't found in any management textbook. It's not a strategy or a technique. It's simply being present. I'm talking about getting out from behind your desk, rolling up your sleeves, and working alongside your team.

When I was managing hotels at the property level, I always kept a chef's coat hanging in my office. Now, let me be clear—I'm no chef. My culinary skills are limited to not burning toast. But that chef's coat wasn't about my cooking abilities. It was about being ready to jump in and help wherever I was needed.

During busy times in the kitchen, I'd put on that coat and help with plating or washing dishes. In the restaurant, I'd bus tables or run food. At the front desk, I'd help check guests in during rush times.

One evening, we had a big event in our ballroom. The restaurant was full, and we were short-staffed in the kitchen. I put on my chef's coat and headed to the kitchen, ready to help in any way I could. The looks on our kitchen staff's faces were priceless—a mix of surprise and amusement.

"Boss, no offense, but please don't touch the food," the sous chef said with a laugh. Instead, he put me to work organizing the plating line and running completed dishes to the servers. It wasn't glamorous work, but it made a difference. More importantly, it showed the team that I was willing to get my hands dirty (figuratively speaking—food safety is important!) alongside them.

The team got a kick out of seeing me in that chef's coat. It became a running joke—whenever I showed up in the kitchen wearing it, someone inevitably shouted, "Look out, Gordon Ramsay's here!" But beneath the laughter, there was a deeper appreciation. They knew that when things got tough, I wouldn't just delegate from afar—I'd be right there with them, doing whatever needed to be done.

This reminds me of something Don Fox, the retired CEO of Firehouse Subs, once told me: "Your team's ability to watch you far exceeds your ability to watch them." It's an observation that perfectly captures why being present and leading by example is so crucial. Don didn't just understand this principle—he built his entire leadership philosophy around it, encapsulated in what he playfully called his LMAO formula:

L — Lead by Example
M — Mission Orders (don't micro-manage)
A — Accountability
O — Optimistic Leadership

Don always gets a chuckle from his audience when sharing this acronym, and jokes, "Yes, I realize you all know what LMAO stands for . . . and that's the point—you have to have fun!" His ability to combine serious leadership principles with humor exemplifies another important aspect of being present as a leader: authenticity.

This LMAO formula reinforces everything I learned about present leadership throughout my career. When I put on that chef's coat, I wasn't just helping during busy times—I was leading by example. When I trusted my team to make decisions without micromanaging, I was practicing mission orders (let people do the job you hired and trained them to do). When I stood alongside them during challenges, I was demonstrating accountability. And by maintaining a positive presence even during difficult times, I was showing optimism.

Being present is about being mentally and emotionally available to your team. It's about really listening when they speak, being attuned to the mood of your workplace, and being ready to offer support or guidance when it's needed.

I made it a point to do regular "walk-arounds" throughout the hotel. Not formal inspections, but casual check-ins where I could chat with staff, ask how things were going, and get a feel for the day-to-day operations. These walks often revealed issues or opportunities that I might have missed if I'd stayed in my office.

One day during a walk-around, I noticed that our laundry team seemed stressed. After chatting with them, I discovered that one of our washing machines had been acting up, causing delays and extra work. While the maintenance team was aware of the issue, it hadn't been given the necessary priority. Because I was there and took the time to understand their challenges, I was able to escalate the situation immediately. Not only did we get the machine fixed promptly, but the laundry team was incredibly grateful that someone had finally heard their concerns and taken action. This small victory strengthened our relationship and reinforced the importance of being present and responsive to our team's needs. Being a present leader also means being available when your team needs you. I always told my staff that my door was open, and I meant it. Whether it was a work-related issue or a personal problem, I wanted them to know they could come to me.

But being present as a leader goes beyond just being physically there or having an open-door policy. It's about taking responsibility, especially when things go wrong. And in the hospitality industry, things can and do go wrong, often in ways that impact the most basic guest expectations.

One morning we arrived at the hotel to discover the hot water boilers had gone out overnight, a night that just so happened to be sold out. When you stay in a hotel, there are certain basics you absolutely expect—a clean room, a comfortable bed, and yes, hot water for your morning shower. It's not a luxury; it's a fundamental expectation. And we were about to disappoint every single guest in our hotel.

As the first complaints started coming in, it would have been easy to hide in my office, letting the front desk team take the brunt of guest frustrations. After all, this wasn't the first time I'd dealt with this issue—unfortunately, it's a situation that occurs more often than any hotelier cares to admit. But that's exactly when your team needs to see you out front, taking responsibility and facing challenges head-on.

I positioned myself in the lobby, intercepting guests before they could reach the front desk. I knew every minute of their morning routine had been disrupted, and I wanted them to see that their issue was important enough for the general manager to be personally involved.

"I'm Ryan, the general manager," I'd say. "I want to personally apologize for the lack of hot water this morning. Our maintenance team is working on the boilers right now, and I'm here to answer any questions and help however I can."

Some guests were understanding, others less so—and I couldn't blame them. A cold shower isn't how anyone wants to start their day. But by being present, by taking ownership of the situation, we were able to turn many potentially hostile confrontations into more productive conversations.

This wasn't about passing the buck or making excuses. It was about showing our team that when things get tough, leadership doesn't hide. We stand with our people, we face challenges together, and we take responsibility for finding solutions.

The situation was far from ideal, but something interesting happened. As guests saw me and other managers working alongside the staff, actively addressing the problem rather than avoiding it, their anger began to dissipate. Some even commented later about how they appreciated seeing the management team actively involved in handling the crisis.

This reinforced for me several important aspects of taking responsibility as a leader, even when—especially when—things go wrong that aren't directly your fault. It's easy to think, "Well, I didn't break the boiler," or "This is a maintenance issue." The true test of leadership comes in how you handle these inevitable crises. By taking responsibility, you accomplish several important things:

1 You set an example for your team. You show them that when things go wrong, the response should be "How can we fix this?" not "Whose fault is this?"

2 You create a unified front. There's no "us vs. them" mentality when the leader is right there in the trenches with the team.

3 You gain respect. Your team sees that you're willing to face challenges head-on rather than hide behind your title or office door.

4 You maintain focus on solutions. When you take responsibility, you shift the energy from blame to problem-solving.

5 You build trust with your customers or clients. They see that you're committed to making things right, no matter what.

This "we're all in this together" mentality is crucial for building a strong, cohesive team. It's about fostering a culture where everyone, from the highest-ranking manager to the newest entry-level employee, feels equally responsible for the success of the organization.

I've found that this approach not only helps in crisis situations but also in day-to-day operations. When your team knows that you'll be there with them, taking responsibility and working alongside them when things get tough, they're more likely to give their all every day.

For instance, after the hot water incident, I noticed a marked change in how our team approached problems. Instead of immediately calling for a manager when something went wrong, they started to take more initiative in finding solutions themselves. They knew that if they needed backup, I'd be there, but they also felt empowered to handle situations on their own.

This shift created a more proactive, solution-oriented culture throughout the hotel. It wasn't about avoiding responsibility or passing the buck—it was about everyone taking ownership of our guests' experience.

To foster this kind of environment, here are some strategies I've found effective:

- **Be visible:** Make sure your team sees you regularly, not just during crises. Be present in their day-to-day work environment.

- **Get your hands dirty:** Don't be afraid to do the work alongside your team. It builds respect and gives you a better understanding of their challenges.

- **Take responsibility publicly:** When things go wrong, be the first to step up and take responsibility. Don't throw your team under the bus, even if the mistake wasn't directly your fault.

- **Celebrate collective wins:** When things go well, make sure to credit the team. Use "we" language to reinforce the idea that you're all in this together.

- **Support risk-taking:** Encourage your team to take initiative and assure them that you'll have their back if things don't go as planned.

- **Share the tough times:** Be transparent about challenges the organization is facing. Involve your team in finding solutions.

- **Learn together:** When mistakes happen, focus on learning from them as a team rather than assigning blame.

To be a present leader, you must be fully engaged, take responsibility, and create a culture where everyone feels part of a unified team working towards a common goal.

It's not always easy. There will be days when you'd rather stay in your office and delegate from afar. There will be times when taking responsibility for a failure that wasn't directly your fault feels unfair. But that's the price of leadership. And it's a price worth paying.

When you roll up your sleeves and take responsibility—when you show your team that you're with them through thick and thin—you create a team that's resilient, united, and ready for any challenge. You create a culture where people don't just come to work—they come to be part of something bigger than themselves.

It's not about titles or corner offices. It's about being there, really being there, for your team. It's about creating an environment where everyone feels valued, supported, and part of a collective mission.

So, keep that chef's coat handy. Be ready to jump in where you're needed. Take responsibility, even when it's tough. Because when you do, you're not just being a boss—you're being a leader. And that makes all the difference in the world.

Reflection Question: When was the last time you worked alongside your team in their day-to-day tasks? What insights did you gain, or what might you learn if you haven't done this recently?

CHAPTER 11

Authentic Leadership: Understanding Your Team's True Value

Understanding and appreciating the diversity of your team is crucial for effective leadership. This isn't just about recognizing different ethnicities or backgrounds—it's about understanding the unique perspectives, experiences, and circumstances of each team member. And sometimes, the importance of this understanding is highlighted by leaders who get it wrong.

I once took over a hotel that was being managed by possibly the worst leader I ever had to manage—let's call her Linda. Linda came to work every day in designer suits that probably cost more than what some of our entry-level staff made in a month. She drove a luxury car and often parked in the front drive for all to see.

Now, there's nothing inherently wrong with being successful or enjoying the fruits of your labor. The problem was that Linda seemed oblivious to how this came across to the rest of the team (or she just didn't care), many of whom were struggling to make ends meet.

As I was visiting the hotel one day, I overheard a conversation between two housekeepers. One was saying how she had to choose between buying new shoes for her kid or paying the electric bill that month. The next day, Linda was meeting her personal stylist in the lobby to review her upcoming season's wardrobe—the consultant's fee alone exceeded that housekeeper's monthly salary.

The disconnect was remarkable. The staff didn't respect Linda, not because of her success, but because of her lack of awareness and empathy. She didn't seem to understand or care about the realities of their lives.

This reminded me of the importance of knowing your audience—your team. It's about being aware of the diverse backgrounds, experiences, and challenges of the people you lead.

As a leader, I made it a priority to understand the realities of my team's lives. I knew that we had single parents struggling with childcare, team members working second jobs to make ends meet, and others dealing with health issues or caring for elderly parents.

This knowledge helped me become a more effective and empathetic leader. When I knew that someone was working a second job, I could be more understanding about scheduling. When I was aware that a team member was dealing with a family health crisis, I could offer support and flexibility.

I also created opportunities for the team to share their diverse perspectives and experiences. We started having monthly potluck lunches where people could bring dishes from their cultural backgrounds. It was a simple thing, but it opened up conversations and fostered understanding among the team.

We also implemented a "Day in the Life" program, where team members could shadow someone in a different department. This not only helped with cross-training but also gave everyone a better appreciation for the challenges and contributions of their colleagues.

Knowing your team also means understanding the strength that diversity brings. Different perspectives lead to better problem-solving and innovation. A diverse team can better understand and serve a diverse customer base.

As we were brainstorming ideas to improve our guest experience, a front desk agent who had recently immigrated from the Philippines suggested we offer a selection of international power adapters for guests to borrow. It was such a simple idea, but one that many of us, used to domestic travel, hadn't considered. It ended up being hugely popular with our international guests.

As a leader, it's your job to create an environment where this diversity is not just accepted, but celebrated. This means being aware of your own biases, actively seeking out different perspectives, and ensuring that all voices are heard and valued.

But knowing your team isn't just about understanding diversity. It's also about recognizing the strengths and expertise each team member brings to the table *because* of their diversity. Great leaders understand that they don't need to be the smartest person in the room. In fact, if you are the smartest person in the room, you're probably in the wrong room.

This lesson was driven home to me when I worked with an above property corporate asset manager—let's call him Patrick—who epitomized the opposite of this principle. Patrick had never worked a day in his life in a hotel, yet he constantly talked to the general managers and operations leaders as if he were the ultimate expert in hospitality.

Patrick's ideas were often terrible, showing a clear lack of understanding of the day-to-day realities of running a hotel. But what made it worse was his refusal to listen to the actual experts—the people who had years of experience in the industry.

At one point, Patrick tried to school me on customer service. Now, I don't claim to know everything about customer service, but I had written a book on the subject and was sitting next to a general manager who was a professor of guest service at a local university. Yet Patrick, who had never worked in a customer-facing role in his life, spoke to us as if we were novices.

The result? No one respected Patrick. Great people at the property and corporate level left the company because of his attitude. His insistence on being the "smartest person in the room" not only hindered innovation and growth but actually drove away talent.

Patrick reinforced for me the importance of humility (or in his case, the lack thereof) in leadership. Good leaders surround themselves with great people—people who are smarter, more experienced, or more skilled in various areas. These leaders create an environment where team members feel valued and heard.

As a general manager, I made it a point to hire people who were experts in their areas—people who knew more than I did about their specific roles. I had a head of housekeeping who could tell you the most efficient way to clean a room down to the second. My chef knew more about food costs and menu engineering than I ever could. My director of sales could recite market trends and competitive analyses off the top of her head.

My job wasn't to know more than them—it was to create an environment where they could apply their expertise effectively. I made sure to regularly seek their input, to defer to their judgment in their areas of expertise, and to publicly recognize their contributions.

This approach had several benefits:

1 It led to better decision-making. By drawing on the diverse expertise of the team, we made more informed choices.

2 It increased employee engagement. Team members felt valued for their knowledge and skills, which motivated them to contribute more.

3 It fostered a culture of continuous learning. When people see that expertise is valued, they're more motivated to develop their skills further.

4 It improved retention. People are more likely to stay with a company where they feel their expertise is recognized and utilized.

5 It allowed me to focus on my role as a leader. Instead of trying to be an expert in everything, I could focus on setting the vision, removing obstacles, and supporting my team.

Your job as a leader isn't to have all the answers. It's to ask the right questions, to create an environment where your team feels comfortable sharing their knowledge and ideas, and to synthesize all of this input into a cohesive strategy.

Here are some strategies for embracing this approach:

- **Hire for complementary skills:** Look for people who are strong in areas where you're weak. This creates a more well-rounded team.

- **Regularly seek input:** Make it a habit to ask for your team's thoughts and ideas. This not only leads to better solutions but also shows that you value their expertise.

- **Give credit generously:** When a team member's idea leads to success, make sure to publicly acknowledge their contribution.

- **Create opportunities for sharing knowledge:** This could be through formal training sessions, informal lunch-and-learns, or mentoring programs.

- **Be open about what you don't know:** It's okay to say, "I don't know, but let's find out together." This vulnerability can actually increase your team's respect for you.

- **Celebrate diverse perspectives:** When team members disagree, see it as an opportunity for rich discussion rather than a problem to be solved.

Knowing your team means more than just understanding their diverse backgrounds and experiences. It means recognizing and valuing the unique expertise each person brings to the table. It means creating an environment where this diversity of thought and experience is seen as a strength, not a challenge to be managed.

When you know your team—its strengths, challenges, and expertise—you can create a more innovative, engaged, and successful organization. Think of yourself as a conductor blending an orchestra of talents to create something beautiful.

So, take the time to know your team. Understand their diverse perspectives. Value their unique expertise. Create an environment where everyone feels heard and appreciated. Because when you do, you're not just being a good boss—you're being a great leader. And great leaders know that the strength of their organization lies not in their own knowledge, but in the collective wisdom and diverse talents of their team.

Reflection Question: How effectively are you leveraging the diverse perspectives and experiences within your team, and what voices might you be unintentionally overlooking?

CHAPTER 12

Cross-Generational Leadership: Bridging Gaps Through Positive Practice

I was in a meeting with Don Fox, the retired CEO of Firehouse Subs I mentioned previously, when he shared something that perfectly captured one of the biggest challenges—and opportunities—in leadership today. We were discussing seasoned managers' common complaint about "kids these days" not wanting to work.

"You know what really frustrates me?" he said, leaning forward in his chair. "It's when I hear leaders—especially experienced ones who should know better—saying that this generation is lazy or doesn't want to work. Every generation has said that about the generation that came after them. Every single one. And every single time, they've been wrong."

He continued, his passion for leadership evident in his voice. "The reality is, if we're not getting the results we want from our younger team members, that's not on them—that's on us as leaders. We need to be more motivating and better leaders."

This conversation with Don reminded me of something I had learned early in my career about leading across generations. I was a young general manager, and like many leaders, I initially struggled to connect with team members from different age groups. Some were old enough to be my parents, others young enough to be my children. Each seemed to have different expectations, communication styles, and views about work.

Early on, I decided to eat in the employee break room rather than in the hotel restaurant. The restaurant offered a more refined setting and networking opportunities, but eating in the break room helped me dismantle barriers between management and staff. It's where I learned about our housekeepers' grandchildren, where our maintenance team shared stories about their weekend projects renovating their home or helping a neighbor build a fence, and where our younger staff members talked about what colleges they were applying to. These daily interactions broke down generational barriers in ways that no formal program ever could.

But eating in the break room was just the beginning. I learned that effective cross-generational leadership requires a deliberate approach to understanding and connecting with people at every stage of life. Here's what I discovered works:

First, abandon any preconceived notions about generational stereotypes. Just as Don pointed out, the idea that any generation is "lazy" or "entitled" is not only wrong—it's counterproductive. Instead, focus on understanding the unique perspectives and experiences that shape each generation's approach to work.

I once had a conversation with Alyiah, one of our youngest front desk agents. She had suggested creating Instagram-worthy photo opportunities in our lobby. My first instinct was to dismiss it as frivolous. But when I took the time to listen, I realized she understood something crucial about modern guest expectations that I had missed. Her "millennial perspective" wasn't a liability—it was an asset that helped us stay relevant in a changing market.

Similarly, I learned to value the stability and deep institutional knowledge that our more seasoned team members brought to the table. Chuck, our veteran maintenance supervisor, might not have been active on social media, but his understanding of our building's systems and his relationship with long-term guests were invaluable. Chuck's deep understanding of our building's systems meant he could diagnose and fix HVAC issues within hours, while outside contractors might have needed days just to understand the equipment's quirks. But his true value went beyond technical skills—it was his authentic connections with long-term guests that set our service apart.

Take Mrs. Anderson, a monthly business traveler who stayed with us for over a decade. Chuck remembered her precise temperature preference of 72 degrees and would adjust her room before each arrival. He maintained detailed notes on her preferred room's maintenance schedule, ensuring everything from shower pressure to window seals met her standards.

His institutional memory and attention to detail created the kind of personalized experiences that turn first-time visitors into loyal guests—the type of service excellence that marketing dollars simply can't buy.

The key was creating an environment where different generational strengths could complement each other rather than conflict. We started a two-way mentoring program where younger team members helped their older colleagues with technology, while seasoned employees shared their years of customer service wisdom.

Communication proved to be another crucial area where generational differences required thoughtful leadership. While our older team members often preferred face-to-face conversations, younger staff members were more comfortable with text messages and digital platforms. We embraced this diversity by creating multiple channels for sharing information and getting feedback. One of the most successful initiatives was launching an internal Facebook page for our staff. It became a vibrant space where we could post photos, celebrate achievements, and communicate important updates in a way that felt natural to our younger team members while encouraging our more experienced staff to engage with new technology.

But perhaps the most important lesson I learned about cross-generational leadership was this: regardless of age, everyone wants to feel valued, heard, and understood. The methods of showing appreciation might need to vary—a handwritten note might mean more to one team member, while public recognition on our digital platforms might resonate more with another—but the fundamental human need for recognition transcends generational boundaries.

I'll never forget the day one of our younger housekeepers, Jamie, came to me in tears. She had just received a handwritten thank-you note from Eleanor, our most experienced room inspector, who was known for her exacting standards. "I didn't think she even noticed my work," Jamie said. "But she wrote that my attention to detail reminds her of herself when she was starting out."

That moment exemplified what positive cross-generational leadership can achieve. It's not about forcing different generations to conform to one way of working—it's about creating bridges of understanding and appreciation that allow everyone to bring their best selves to work.

Don Fox's wisdom about leadership responsibility rings especially true when it comes to managing across generations. If we're not getting the results we want, we need to look first at our own leadership approach. Are we making assumptions based on age? Are we failing to communicate effectively? Are we missing opportunities to leverage diverse perspectives?

The reality is, today's workforce is more generationally diverse than ever before. We might have team members from four or even five different generations working side by side. This diversity can be our greatest strength—but only if we lead in a way that bridges gaps rather than reinforces them.

Positive leadership isn't about treating everyone the same—it's about treating everyone as individuals while creating an environment where differences become strengths rather than sources of conflict. When we get this right, we create teams that don't just tolerate generational diversity—they thrive because of it.

Reflection Question: How are you leveraging the unique strengths of each generation in your team, and what assumptions might be holding you back from fully engaging with team members of different ages?

CHAPTER 13

Positive Communication: The Language of Great Leaders

As a general manager, I worked with a manager named Frank who had a knack for turning every conversation into a negative experience. Whether he was giving feedback, discussing goals, or even praising someone's work, his words always seemed to leave people feeling deflated rather than motivated.

I was at a staff meeting where Frank was discussing our recent customer satisfaction scores. We had improved significantly over the past quarter, but instead of celebrating this win, Frank focused entirely on the areas where we were still falling short. By the end of the meeting, the team looked completely demoralized, despite the fact that we had actually made great progress.

This experience taught me a valuable lesson about the power of positive communication. It's not just about what you say, but how you say it. But more than that, it taught me about the importance of vision and optimism in leadership communication.

Great leaders understand that their words have the power to shape reality. They know that the language they use can either inspire their team to reach for the stars or resign themselves to mediocrity. This is why the most effective leaders I've encountered all share a common trait: they lead with vision and optimism.

For example, a few years after my experience with Frank, I had the privilege of working with a leader who was the complete opposite. Betsy had an extraordinary ability to paint a vivid picture of the future that made everyone excited to be a part of it.

During my tenure with Betsy, our hotel was undergoing a major renovation. It was a difficult time—we were operating at reduced capacity, dealing with noise complaints, and stretching our staff thin. But Betsy's communication throughout this period was a masterclass in positive, visionary leadership.

In our team meetings, instead of dwelling on the current challenges, Betsy transported us to the future. "Imagine six months from now," she'd say, "when we unveil our newly renovated property. Picture the looks on our guests' faces as they walk into our stunning new lobby. Think about the pride you'll feel knowing you were part of the team that made this transformation happen."

She didn't ignore the current difficulties—she acknowledged them honestly. But she always framed them within the context of our larger vision. "Yes, we're facing some tough days," she'd say, "but every challenge we overcome is bringing us one step closer to our goal. We're not just renovating a hotel—we're creating a space where people will make memories for years to come. And you are all an essential part of making that vision a reality."

The impact of Betsy's communication style was profound. When guest complaints about construction noise would come in, she'd look for ways to minimize disruption instead of just subscribing to, "It is to be expected."

"This feedback is a gift," she'd say, turning each issue into an opportunity to improve our renovation process. After one guest expressed frustration about dust in the hallways, Betsy worked with housekeeping to develop new cleaning protocols, and additional air purifiers were installed. The team began to see challenges not as setbacks but as chances to enhance our future guest experience.

Even on the toughest days, the team remained motivated and engaged. We weren't just slogging through a difficult renovation—we were building the future of our hotel. This sense of purpose and vision made all the difference.

Great leaders don't just react to the present—they actively shape the future through their words and actions. They understand that their team needs more than just instructions or feedback—they need a compelling vision to work towards.

But having a vision isn't enough. Great leaders also know how to set clear expectations and inspire their team to meet them. They understand that people rise to the level of expectations set for them, so they consistently set the bar high while providing the support needed to reach it.

I learned this lesson early in my leadership journey, and it has shaped my approach ever since. When I took over as general manager of a struggling property, one of the first things I did was gather the leadership team for a vision-setting session.

"I want us to be the number one hotel in customer satisfaction in our region within one year," I announced. I could see the shock on some faces—we were currently ranked near the bottom. "I know this sounds ambitious," I continued, "but I've seen what this team is capable of. We have the skills, the dedication, and the heart to make this happen. And here's how we're going to do it . . ."

I then laid out a clear, step-by-step plan for how we would achieve this goal. I set specific, measurable targets for each department. Front desk would focus on reducing check-in times from seven to four minutes while maintaining genuine guest connections. Housekeeping would work to raise room cleanliness scores from 85 percent to 95 percent, ensuring every guest walked into a spotless room. But more importantly, I painted a picture of what success looked like—not just for the hotel, but for each team member personally.

"Imagine the sense of pride you'll feel," I said, "when you can tell your friends and family that you work at the top-rated hotel in the region. Think about the opportunities this will create for all of us as our reputation grows."

By setting a clear vision and high expectations, and by tying it to personal growth and pride, I was able to ignite a fire in the team. We didn't just meet our goal—we exceeded it, becoming the top-rated hotel in our region in just nine months.

Exceeding our goal reinforced for me the power of positive, visionary communication. When leaders communicate with optimism and clarity, they can inspire their teams to achieve things they never thought possible.

But it's not just about the big vision talks. Positive communication needs to be a constant, day-to-day practice. Here are some strategies I've found effective:

- **Start with appreciation:** Before diving into any topic, start by expressing appreciation for your team's efforts. This sets a positive tone for the conversation.

- **Frame challenges as opportunities:** Instead of saying, "We have a problem with customer complaints," try, "We have an opportunity to significantly improve our customer experience."
- **Use "we" language:** This reinforces that you're all in this together. It's not about you giving orders but about the team working towards a common goal.
- **Be specific with praise:** Don't just say, "Good job." Explain exactly what was good and why it matters. This not only makes the praise more meaningful but also reinforces the behaviors you want to see.
- **Ask empowering questions:** Instead of always providing solutions, ask questions that stimulate creative thinking. Ask, "How do you think we could improve this process?" or "What ideas do you have for reaching this goal?"
- **Communicate progress regularly:** Keep the team updated on movement towards goals. Celebrate milestones along the way to maintain momentum and motivation.
- **Be transparent and honest:** Share both good news and bad news. Your team will appreciate your authenticity, and it will build trust.
- **End with inspiration:** Always try to end conversations on a positive, forward-looking note. Remind the team of the vision you're working towards and express confidence in their ability to achieve it.

As a leader, your words have immense power. They can inspire or discourage, motivate or deflate. By consistently communicating with positivity, vision, and optimism, you create an environment where people are excited to come to work each day, where they feel valued and motivated to give their best.

Positive communication isn't just about making people feel good. It's a strategic tool that can drive real business results. When people feel inspired and valued, they're more creative, more productive, and more committed to the organization's success.

I've seen this play out time and time again in my career. Teams led with positive, visionary communication consistently outperform those that aren't. They're more resilient in the face of challenges, more innovative in their problem-solving, and more dedicated to delivering exceptional results.

For example, a few years ago, I was brought in to turn around a hotel that was struggling with low employee morale and poor customer reviews. The previous management had relied heavily on negative reinforcement—pointing out mistakes, criticizing performance, and generally creating a culture of fear.

My first step was to completely overhaul the communication style. We instituted daily team huddles that always started with recognition of great performance. We created a wall of fame where we posted positive customer reviews and celebrated the team members mentioned in them. In every interaction, I linked our daily work to our larger vision of becoming the most welcoming, guest-focused hotel in the city. Within six months, our employee satisfaction scores doubled. Our customer reviews improved dramatically, with guests frequently mentioning how friendly and helpful our staff was. Revenue and profitability increased significantly.

All of this stemmed from a shift in how we communicated. By leading with vision, optimism, and positivity, we were able to unleash the full potential of our team.

As you think about your own leadership communication, reflect on these questions:

- How often do you communicate your vision for the future to your team?
- Do your words inspire and motivate, or do they simply instruct and correct?
- Are you setting high expectations and expressing confidence in your team's ability to meet them?
- How can you infuse more positivity and optimism into your daily interactions?

Every interaction is an opportunity to inspire, motivate, and move your team closer to your shared vision. Use your words wisely. Communicate with positivity, clarity, and purpose. When you do, you're not just sharing information—you're shaping the future of your organization and the lives of the people you lead.

That's the power of positive communication. That's the language of great leaders. Moreover, it's a skill that, with practice and intention, we can all develop. So go forth and communicate with vision, with optimism, and with the knowledge that your words have the power to transform your team and your organization. The future you envision is waiting to be spoken into existence. It's time to use the language of great leaders to make it a reality.

Reflection Question: Think about your most recent challenging conversation with a team member. How could you have reframed your message more positively while still addressing the core issue?

CHAPTER 14

Empowerment Through Trust: Letting Your Team Shine

Earlier in this book, I mentioned how much I dislike the P word: policy. Too often, policies become barriers preventing our people from doing what's right for the customer. Policies can become excuses for not going above and beyond, shields to hide behind rather than guidelines to work from.

Let me share a powerful experience that perfectly illustrates what happens when policies prevent employees from being empowered. Not long after taking over a hotel in Boca Raton, while still establishing my empowerment guidelines, I arrived one morning to find our director of sales waiting to speak with me, visibly upset. She shared a troubling situation from the previous night: one of our VIP guests from the hotel's million-dollar top account had attempted to check in but had lost her wallet containing all her identification and credit cards.

Despite the front desk agent having the guest's complete history right in front of him—showing she had stayed with us over fifty times that year, represented our top account, had VIP status, and even had stored credit card information—the front desk agent remained rigidly focused on the "policy" requiring physical ID and credit card presentation. Instead of recognizing an opportunity to deliver exceptional service, he turned away a valued guest who ended up staying at our competitor across the street.

Think about the devastating impact of this policy-driven decision. Not only did we lose that immediate guest stay, but we ultimately lost the entire account—a million-dollar relationship that, as far as I know, remains with that competitor to this day. With proper empowerment, this situation could have played out very differently:

1 The agent could have verified the guest's identity through her extensive stay history and stored information.
2 He could have documented the situation and made special arrangements for proper documentation the next day.
3 At the very least, he could have escalated the situation to find a creative solution rather than simply saying "no."

Instead, rigid adherence to policy turned what could have been a moment of exceptional service into a catastrophic loss of business. This is exactly why I believe in empowering our teams to think beyond policy and focus on solving guest problems. Sometimes doing the right thing means knowing when to be flexible with our guidelines to serve our guests' needs.

Let me contrast this with a story about Jason, the young man who taught me the power of saying, "Thanks for coming in today." Well, he also taught me something awesome about what real empowerment looks like.

One snowy night, a family pulled into our hotel well after midnight. They were exhausted, traveling with young children, and the weather was getting worse by the minute. When they approached the front desk, Jason had to give them news no hotel employee wants to deliver—we were completely sold out.

Now, in many hotels, this is where the story likely ends. "Sorry, we're full," is a common response, typically followed by directions to the next closest hotel. That would have been the "policy" answer. But Jason didn't think in terms of policies—he thought in terms of people.

Instead of turning the family away, Jason got creative. He knew we had a small meeting room that wasn't being used that night. Without hesitation, he told the family, "I think I can help you." He proceeded to transform that meeting room into a cozy temporary bedroom. He gathered extra blankets and pillows from housekeeping, set up a comfortable sleeping area, and even found some coloring books and crayons for the kids.

Jason turned what could have been a terrible night for this family into an adventure. He framed it as a fun "indoor camping experience" for the kids, making them feel special rather than like they were getting a makeshift solution. He didn't just solve their problem—he created a memorable experience.

The family was so touched by Jason's efforts that they later wrote a letter praising his creativity and kindness. They didn't talk about the unusual sleeping arrangements or the fact that they spent the night in a meeting room. Instead, they raved about how Jason had gone above and beyond to help them when they were tired and worried. This letter would later become a cornerstone piece in Jason's nomination for the Rose Award—the highest honor someone in Cincinnati's hospitality market can receive, presented by Cincy Hospitality Professionals. When Jason won this prestigious award, it served as a powerful reminder of what's possible when we truly empower our teams.

This is what empowerment looks like in action. Jason didn't need to check with a manager. He didn't hide behind policies. He saw a problem, knew he had the authority to solve it, and took initiative to create a solution that not only met the family's basic need for shelter but turned a potentially negative situation into a positive memory.

The difference between Jason's response and the overnight front desk agent's response illustrates a fundamental truth about empowerment: it's not just about giving people permission to make decisions—it's about creating an environment where they feel confident and supported in making creative choices to help others.

So how do we create this kind of environment? It starts with trust, but it's more than just saying, "I trust you." It's about demonstrating that trust consistently and backing it up with support when team members take initiative.

When I share Jason's story, people often ask, "But weren't you worried about liability issues with letting people sleep in a meeting room?" Or, "What if something had gone wrong?" These are valid questions, but they reveal exactly the kind of policy-first thinking that kills exceptional service.

Instead of leading with, "What could go wrong?" we should be asking, "How can we make this right?" That's the mindset I worked to instill in my teams. "I'd rather apologize for something you did trying to help a guest than explain why we didn't try at all."

This doesn't mean throwing caution to the wind. It means creating guidelines rather than rigid policies. Here's how we approached it:

1 **Focus on the objective, not the rules:** Our objective was taking care of our guests. That's different from simply following policies.

2 **Create safety nets:** Let your team know that if they make a decision in good faith to help a guest, you'll back them up—even if it doesn't work out perfectly.

3 **Celebrate creative solutions:** When team members find innovative ways to solve problems, share these stories widely. Make heroes out of people who think outside the box.

4 **Learn from every situation:** Whether the outcome is positive or negative, use each instance of employee initiative as a learning opportunity for the entire team.

One morning in our daily huddle, I shared Jason's story about the family in the meeting room. Instead of focusing on the potential risks or policy violations, we discussed what made his solution so perfect: it solved the immediate problem, created a positive experience, and showed genuine care for the guests.

This led to what I call the "domino effect of empowerment." Other team members started sharing their own stories of creative problem-solving. Our bell staff figured out a system for helping guests get their cars out of our snowed-in parking lot. Housekeeping created a "forgot it" box of commonly left-behind items they could provide to guests. The maintenance team developed a proactive system for checking on elderly guests during power outages.

The key was that none of these initiatives required lengthy approval processes or policy reviews. Our team members felt empowered to see a need and fill it.

When I took over a new hotel as the general manager, I made empowerment through trust a cornerstone of my leadership style. I believed that if I hired the right people and gave them the tools and authority to do their jobs well, they would exceed my expectations.

One of the first things I did was to inform the team they could do anything it took to ensure an upset customer left the hotel satisfied. This meant that if a guest had an issue, any staff member could offer compensation or upgrades without having to get manager approval. It was a bit scary at first—I worried about potential abuse or over-spending. But what I found was that when given this responsibility, the team became more judicious and thoughtful about how they used it.

Taylor, a front desk agent, told me about a guest who had a terrible day—lost luggage, delayed flights, and a mix-up with their reservation. Instead of just offering a standard upgrade or discount, Taylor arranged a surprise in-room dinner for the guest and their family. The guest was so touched by this gesture that they became a loyal customer, returning to our hotel whenever they were in town.

Empowerment isn't just about allowing people to make decisions—it's also about giving them the tools and knowledge they need to make good decisions. We implemented a comprehensive training program that went beyond just teaching people how to do their jobs. We taught them about the business as a whole—how the hotel operated, what our financial goals were, and how their role contributed to the bigger picture.

This holistic understanding allowed team members to make decisions that weren't just good for the immediate situation but good for the hotel overall. For example, our housekeeping staff, understanding the importance of positive reviews to our business, started leaving personalized welcome notes for guests. It was a small gesture that cost nothing but had a big impact on guest satisfaction.

Empowering your team doesn't mean abdicating your responsibility as a leader. Instead, it means finding the right balance between giving freedom and providing guidance. I made sure to have regular check-ins with team members—not to micromanage, but to offer support and ensure they had what they needed to succeed.

I also made it clear that it was okay to make mistakes. In fact, I encouraged calculated risk-taking. When someone tried something new that didn't quite work out, instead of punishing them, we treated it as a learning opportunity. This created a culture where people weren't afraid to innovate and take initiative.

Your job as a leader isn't to have all the answers or to control every aspect of your operation. It's to create an environment where your team can thrive, innovate, and exceed even their own expectations. When you empower through trust, you're not just building a better team—you're building a better business.

Reflection Question: What's the most significant decision you're currently unwilling to delegate, and what steps could you take to trust and empower your team to handle it?

CHAPTER 15

The Next Generation of Positive Leaders: Developing Your Team's Leadership Potential

One of our most important responsibilities as leaders is to develop the next generation of leaders. It's not just about managing today's business—it's about building tomorrow's leaders. And sometimes, that means taking chances on people who have the right qualities but might not have the traditional experience. That's exactly what happened with Mari.

I first met Mari when she applied for our front desk manager position. On paper, she had the basic qualifications we were looking for—some supervisory experience, good customer service background, and solid references. But the moment she walked into the interview, I knew there was something special about her. It wasn't just her professional demeanor or her well-prepared responses. It was her energy, her enthusiasm, and most importantly, her natural ability to connect with people.

During that first conversation, Mari didn't just answer questions—she engaged in a genuine dialogue about leadership, guest service, and team development. She had that rare quality that I've come to recognize as true leadership potential: the ability to think beyond the immediate task to see bigger possibilities.

I hired her on the spot.

Within months, Mari had transformed our front desk operations. She had this incredible knack for bringing out the best in her team, for turning everyday interactions into opportunities for growth and development. I watched as she mentored her staff, celebrated their successes, and helped them learn from their mistakes.

But what really impressed me was how she thought about the business as a whole. She wasn't just focused on her department—she was always thinking about how the front desk could better support housekeeping, how they could work more effectively with mainte-nance, how they could enhance the overall guest experience.

That's when I knew Mari was ready for more. Much more.

I called her into my office one day and asked her a question that caught her completely off guard: "How would you feel about becoming our director of operations?"

The look on her face was priceless. "But Ryan," she said, "I've only been here eight months. And I've never managed multiple departments before."

"True," I replied. "But you have something more important than experience—you have talent, drive, and, most importantly, the right attitude. We can teach the technical stuff. We can't teach those other qualities."

This is a philosophy I've held throughout my career: talent and attitude trump experience every time. You can teach someone how to manage a budget, how to create schedules, how to handle operational procedures. But you can't teach someone to care deeply about their team. You can't teach someone to have natural leadership instincts. You can't teach someone to have the right attitude.

Mari accepted the position, and true to form, exceeded all expectations. But I wasn't done pushing her growth yet. A few months later, an opportunity arose that really tested this philosophy.

Our food and beverage director position opened up, and instead of looking for someone with years of restaurant experience, I offered it to Mari. This time, her reaction was even more dramatic.

"Ryan, have you lost your mind?" she laughed nervously. "I've never even worked in a restaurant!"

"No," I agreed, "but you understand people, you know how to lead, and you have an incredible ability to learn quickly. The rest we can teach you."

I won't pretend it was an easy transition. There were moments of uncertainty, times when Mari questioned herself, and times when others questioned my decision. But Mari approached the role with the same dedication, humility, and enthusiasm that had caught my attention in that first interview.

She immersed herself in learning everything she could about food and beverage operations. She spent time in the kitchen, learning from our chef. She worked alongside the servers to understand their challenges. She studied wine lists, menu engineering, and cost control. But most importantly, she brought her natural leadership abilities to a new team, creating the same positive, growth-oriented environment she had built at the front desk.

Within six months, our food and beverage operations were showing significant improvement. Not just in numbers, but in team morale, guest satisfaction, and overall energy. Mari had done what great leaders do—she had made everyone around her better.

When you're developing future leaders, you need to look beyond the obvious. Don't just look at what someone has done—look at what they're capable of doing. Don't just consider their experience—consider their potential.

Here are some key principles I've learned about developing the next generation of positive leaders:

1 **Look for attitude first.**
   Technical skills can be taught. Systems can be learned. Procedures can be memorized. But attitude—that's innate. Look for people who have the following characteristics:

   - A natural desire to learn and grow
   - Genuine care for others
   - Enthusiasm for challenges
   - A positive outlook
   - The ability to connect with people

2 **Create growth opportunities.**
   Don't wait for the perfect position to open up. Look for ways to stretch and develop your high-potential team members:

   - Give them special projects.
   - Let them lead initiatives.
   - Create new roles that leverage their strengths.
   - Cross-train them in different areas.

3 Provide support while allowing struggle.

When you put someone in a stretch position like I did
with Mari, you need to look for ways to support them:

- Be available for guidance and support.
- Allow them to struggle and learn from mistakes.
- Provide resources and training.
- Shield them from unnecessary pressure while they learn.
- Celebrate their successes, no matter how small.

4 Focus on transferable skills.

Great leadership skills transfer across departments
and industries. Look for people who demonstrate the
following:

- Strong communication abilities
- Problem-solving skills
- Emotional intelligence
- Team-building capabilities
- Strategic thinking

5 Be patient with technical learning.

Technical knowledge comes with time and exposure.
What's important is their attitude:

- Willingness to learn
- Ability to ask good questions
- Humility to admit what they don't know
- Drive to master new skills

Trust your instincts. If you see potential in someone, don't let traditional requirements hold you back. Some of the best leaders I've developed were people who didn't fit the conventional mold.

Today, Mari is one of the most successful leaders I know. When I ask her about her journey, she often says, "You saw something in me that I didn't even see in myself."

That's what developing positive leaders is all about—seeing the potential in people and having the courage to help them reach it. It's about looking beyond traditional paths and requirements to identify those special qualities that make great leaders. It's about being willing to take chances on people who have the right attitude and attributes, even if their resume doesn't check all the conventional boxes.

Every great leader started somewhere. Someone had to give them a chance, had to see their potential, had to believe in them. As positive leaders, that's our responsibility—not just to lead today, but to develop the leaders who will carry our organizations into the future.

The next Mari might be sitting right under your nose in your organization. They might not have the perfect resume or the traditional experience. But if they have the right attitude, the right potential, and the right heart for leadership, your job is to find them, develop them, and give them the opportunity to grow.

Ultimately, the true measure of our success as leaders isn't just what we achieve—it's who we help develop along the way. The next generation of positive leaders we help create will carry forward our legacy of positive leadership.

When someone like Mari flourishes and goes on to develop other leaders, we realize that taking a chance on promising people who radiate talent and attitude is one of the most rewarding things a leader can do.

Reflection Question: Who on your team shows leadership potential that you haven't fully developed yet, and what specific opportunities could you create to help them grow?

CHAPTER 16

Measuring What Matters: The ROI of Positive Leadership

Remember Linda? The manager I mentioned earlier who showed up to work in designer suits that cost more than her housekeepers' monthly salaries? Well, there's more to that story—a story that perfectly illustrates how leadership directly impacts not just morale, but every measurable aspect of a business.

Linda wasn't just out of touch with her team's financial realities. Her leadership style was toxic in ways that went far beyond her wardrobe choices. She ruled through intimidation, played favorites, and seemed more interested in wining and dining the local celebrities than taking care of her team or guests. Every day, you could feel the heaviness in the air—a sense of dread and unhappiness that hung over the employees like a dark cloud. The team's spirit was broken, their energy drained before they even started their shifts.

The damage she caused was measurable. During her tenure, six out of every ten employees quit. Customer satisfaction scores plunged to the bottom quartile of our brand. Revenue fell while our competitors' rose. Our profit margins were eaten away by constant recruitment and training costs. Our guest review scores on social media plummeted, with many reviews specifically mentioning "unfriendly staff" and a "negative atmosphere."

Something had to change. There's a correlation between leadership, employee engagement, and business results. An organization's leader sets the tone for everyone in the operation.

I brought in a new manager, Jordyn, who quickly showed she was different from Linda. She led with empathy, recognized her team's contributions, and understood that her role was to serve her team, not lord over them. Most importantly, she created an environment where people wanted to come to work. You could find her walking the property at all hours, from early morning kitchen prep to late-night security rounds, making herself accessible to every shift and every department. Her office door stayed open, but she was rarely in it—she believed in managing by walking around, staying connected to both her team and our guests.

The results came faster than even I expected. Within the first month,

- employees calling off for their shift dropped by 60 percent,
- customer complaints decreased by 50 percent,
- our guest satisfaction scores began trending upward, and
- revenue started climbing.

By the end of the first quarter,

- employee turnover had decreased to 25 percent,
- customer satisfaction scores had moved from the bottom quartile to the top half of our brand,

- revenue was up 15 percent compared to the previous year,
- our profit margins had improved by 8 percent due to reduced turnover and training costs, and
- our social media ratings had improved by 1.5 stars.

This dramatic turnaround illustrates that positive leadership improves soft metrics like "employee happiness" and "positive culture" but also directly affects the bottom line.

Every time an employee quits, it costs a company roughly 1.5 times their annual salary to recruit, hire, and train their replacement. High turnover also affects service quality, team morale, guest satisfaction, and, ultimately, revenue.

However, when employees are engaged and happy at work, they create better guest experiences. Better guest experiences lead to higher satisfaction scores, more repeat business, and more positive reviews. All of these factors directly impact our revenue and profitability.

But here's the key: to measure the ROI of positive leadership, we need to look at both leading and lagging indicators. Lagging indicators are the traditional metrics we've always measured:

- Revenue
- Profit margins
- Market share
- Customer satisfaction scores

Leading indicators, however, tell us where we're headed:

- Employee engagement scores
- Team member satisfaction surveys

- Internal promotion rates
- Employee referral rates
- Training participation rates

In Jordyn's case, we saw the leading indicators improve first. Within weeks, team members were volunteering for extra shifts. Training session attendance doubled. Employees started referring their friends for open positions. These were early signs that the culture was shifting, and the lagging indicators—our financial results—soon followed.

I've developed what I call the "Positive Leadership Metrics Matrix." It looks at four key areas:

1 People Metrics:

- Employee turnover rate
- Internal promotion rate
- Employee engagement scores
- Training completion rates
- Attendance records
- Safety incident reports
- Employee referral rates

2 Guest Metrics:

- Customer satisfaction scores
- Social media ratings
- Guest return rates
- Guest complaint frequency
- Problem resolution satisfaction
- Net promoter score
- Review sentiment analysis

3 Financial Metrics:

- Revenue growth
- Profit margins
- Cost per hire
- Training costs
- Worker's compensation claims
- Operating costs

4 Culture Metrics:

- Employee survey results
- Team participation in optional events
- Cross-department collaboration
- Innovation suggestions
- Community involvement
- Recognition program participation
- Employee wellness program utilization

During a leadership workshop I conducted for a large franchise restaurant company, an executive asked, "How do we measure the impact of positive leadership?"

The answer, I said, lies in how each of the matrices is interconnected: a positive change in one area typically leads to improvements in others. To illustrate, I showed the group how a single positive change in the recognition program at one of our hotels showed up across all four quadrants.

People Metrics:

Employee engagement scores increased by 25 percent.

Guest Metrics:

Customer satisfaction scores improved by 15 percent.

Financial Metrics:

Profit margins increased by 12 percent.

Culture Metrics:

Participation in optional team events doubled.

The executive's eyes lit up as he pictured how these metrics could apply to his stores. This interconnection demonstrates something I've long believed: positive leadership isn't just "nice to have"—it's a crucial business strategy that delivers measurable returns.

While metrics are crucial, we shouldn't let measurements be our sole focus. The overarching goal is to create an environment where people can do their best work and deliver exceptional customer experiences. When we do that right, the numbers follow.

Six months after Jordyn took over and our monthly metrics had skyrocketed, I asked her what sparked the turnaround.

"I never really focus on the numbers directly," she said. "I focus on our people. I make sure they feel valued, supported, and empowered. I create an environment where they want to come to work and do their best. The numbers are just a reflection of that."

She was right. While metrics are important, the ROI of positive leadership isn't just about improving the numbers—it's also about creating an environment where success becomes the natural outcome of how we treat our people and run our business.

While traditional business metrics are important, we also need to measure things that drive those results:

- How many team members feel comfortable bringing new ideas forward
- How often managers recognize and celebrate their team's achievements
- How frequently team members help each other across departments
- How many employees see a future for themselves in the organization

These "soft" metrics might be harder to quantify, but they're often the real drivers of our "hard" business results.

Positive leadership is more than being nice or making people feel good. It creates an environment that drives real, measurable business success.

When we create workplaces where people feel valued, supported, and empowered, we see the results:

- Turnover decreases, reducing our costs.
- Guest satisfaction improves, increasing our revenue.
- Innovation flourishes, driving our growth.
- Productivity increases, improving our profitability.

The ROI of positive leadership is real and measurable. But perhaps the most important return isn't found in any spreadsheet or quarterly report—it's in the lives we impact and the sustainable success we create. When our people thrive, our organization thrives.

Reflection Question: Beyond traditional metrics, what meaningful indicators of positive leadership could you start measuring in your organization, and how would these metrics drive behavior change?

CHAPTER 17

The Balloon Effect: How Positive Leadership Elevates Organizations

Throughout my career, I've seen firsthand how positive leadership can transform not just individuals, but entire organizations. It's like dropping a pebble in a pond—the ripples spread out, affecting every aspect of the business in ways you might not even anticipate. But there's another dimension to this impact that I've come to understand deeply: each person carries an invisible balloon that represents their potential, confidence, and emotional well-being. As leaders, our actions either inflate or deflate these balloons, and when we lift someone up, their elevated spirit creates ripples that extend far beyond any single interaction.

Think about the folks in your own organization for a moment. Each person carries their invisible balloon, constantly being influenced by the environment around them both in their personal and professional lives. Some balloons are full and buoyant, lifting not just their owners but those around them—creating waves of positive energy that spread throughout the organization. Others are damaged, leaking precious energy and enthusiasm through small punctures created by criticism or neglect. Still others hang limp and deflated, their owners having given up hope of ever soaring again.

I witnessed the power of this balloon effect most dramatically when I took over as general manager of a struggling hotel in Cincinnati. The property had been underperforming for years, with low guest satisfaction scores, high employee turnover, and a general sense of malaise that seemed to permeate every aspect of the operation. Walking through the property on my first day, I could almost see the deflated balloons my team members were carrying—their shoulders slumped, their energy low, their confidence damaged by years of negative leadership.

From day one in Cincinnati, I committed to being a leader who inflates rather than deflates. I started by getting to know each team member personally, understanding their strengths, challenges, and aspirations. I instituted the "Thanks for coming in today" greeting I had learned from Jason years before. Each morning, I watched as this simple acknowledgment added a small puff of air to their balloons. We celebrated wins, both big and small. We empowered staff to make decisions and take ownership of guest experiences. Each positive interaction, each word of encouragement, each moment of trust was like adding another breath of air to their balloons.

At first, the changes were small. A housekeeper went out of her way to replace a guest's forgotten toothbrush. A maintenance worker fixed a flickering light in a hallway without being asked. A front desk agent took it upon himself to create a local restaurant guide for guests. These actions were like gentle breezes, slowly lifting the spirits of our team. But more importantly, each lifted balloon created ripples of positivity that touched everyone around them.

Just six months into our transformation, we faced a moment that would test the strength of these newly inflated spirits. A sprinkler pipe directly over our front desk burst, sending water cascading everywhere. In an instant, our primary guest entrance and check-in area became a disaster zone. What happened next showed me just how powerful our cultural transformation had been.

Staff members from every department immediately jumped in to help, their balloons now buoyant enough to rise above the crisis. Housekeepers deployed wet vacs and towels to contain the water. Maintenance workers raced to shut off the water and begin repairs. Our front desk team, their clothes and hair still damp, set up a make-shift desk in a dry area of the lobby and calmly resumed checking in our guests. Our sales team came out and helped greet guests and explain what was happening. No one was told what to do. Everyone saw what needed to be done and did it.

What could have been a catastrophic guest service failure turned into a showcase of our team's resilience and dedication. Guests who witnessed the incident were amazed by how smoothly our team handled the crisis. Instead of complaints, we received compliments about our staff's professionalism and positive attitude in the face of such a challenging situation. The ripples from this event spread far beyond that day, becoming a story that exemplified our new culture.

As our team members' balloons grew stronger and more resilient, they in turn began inflating the balloons of others around them. Guest satisfaction scores started to climb. Employee turnover decreased. We started to see an uptick in repeat guests and positive reviews. About eight months into this transformation, I overheard a conversation between two of our long-time employees. "You know," one said, "I actually look forward to coming to work now. It feels different here."

Their balloons, now full, were lifting not just their own spirits but creating waves of positive energy that touched everyone around them.

The impact spread beyond just guest satisfaction and employee morale. Revenue increased as word spread about our exceptional service. We attracted better talent as people heard about our positive work environment. Our vendor relationships improved as our more positive, solution-oriented approach made us easier to work with. When you create a culture of positivity, appreciation, and empowerment, you build a team that can handle any crisis—even when water is literally raining down on their heads.

Over the course of two years, we went from being in the bottom 20 percent of our brand to the top 5 percent. We were voted one of Cincinnati's best places to work—the only hotel to make the list. And perhaps most importantly, we created a place where both guests and employees wanted to be.

But maintaining this positive environment requires constant attention. Just as a balloon can be deflated by a single prick, a team member's spirit can be damaged by a thoughtless word or action. Through my experience at the Cincinnati hotel, I identified several ways leaders can inadvertently damage their team's balloons:

- Public criticism creates punctures that slowly leak confidence.
- Micromanagement makes the balloon rigid and unable to expand.
- Dismissing ideas adds weight that drags the balloon down.
- Failing to provide resources creates strain that weakens the balloon's material.
- Ignoring achievements reduces the balloon's capacity to hold positive energy.

Conversely, we found specific actions that strengthen and inflate our team's balloons, creating positive ripples throughout the organization:

- Regular recognition adds lift.
- Growth opportunities expand capacity.
- Trust strengthens resilience.
- Clear expectations provide stability.
- Support prevents deflation.
- Celebration increases buoyancy.

The lessons I learned during this transformation have stayed with me throughout my career. I've seen time and time again how positive leadership can turn struggling operations around, elevate good teams to greatness, and create workplaces that people are excited to be a part of.

As leaders, we have the power to shape the environment around us. Every interaction, every decision, every word of encouragement or criticism affects the invisible balloons our team members carry, creating ripples that spread throughout our organization. By choosing positivity, by celebrating our people, by leading with empathy and trust, we can create waves of positive change that transform not just our businesses, but the lives of everyone we touch.

Leadership isn't just about hitting targets or maximizing profits. It's about creating a positive impact—on your team, on your customers, and on your community. When you lead with positivity, when you commit to inflating rather than deflating the spirits of those around you, you're not just building a successful business—you're building a legacy of positive change that can last for years to come.

I encourage you to reflect on your own leadership style. How can you better support and inflate the invisible balloons your team members carry? How can you harness the ripple effect of positive leadership to transform your organization? How can you create an environment where people genuinely look forward to coming to work each day?

The journey of positive leadership is ongoing. There will always be challenges and setbacks. But by committing to these principles, by consistently choosing to be an uplifting force in people's lives, you can create positive change that ripples through your organization and touches countless lives along the way.

It all starts with a simple gesture—a warm greeting, a word of appreciation, a moment of genuine connection. So tomorrow, when you walk into your workplace, take a moment to look each team member in the eye, see the invisible balloons they carry, shake their hand, and say with all sincerity, "Thanks for coming in today." You might be surprised at how that small breath of air creates ripples of positive change throughout your entire organization.

Reflection Question: Think about the invisible balloons your team members carry. What specific actions could you take this week to help inflate them?

The Lasting Impact of Positive Leadership

As we come to the end of our journey through the principles of positive leadership, I'm reminded of a powerful moment that brought home to me just how far-reaching the impact of our actions as leaders can be—how the invisible balloons we help inflate can create ripples that touch lives in ways we never imagined.

Not long after *Thanks for Coming In Today* was published, I was invited to deliver a keynote speech to the leadership team of a well-known casino company. I was excited about the opportunity to share the lessons I'd learned throughout my career, particularly the story of Jason, the young man who had taught me the power of genuine appreciation and positivity in the workplace.

As I stood on the stage, I began to tell Jason's story—how his simple act of greeting everyone with a heartfelt "Thanks for coming in today" had transformed our workplace and become the foundation of my leadership philosophy. I explained how this small gesture of appreciation had lifted the spirits of everyone around him, creating ripples that touched not just our team, but our guests, and ultimately, the success of our hotel.

Suddenly, from the audience, I heard a voice call out, "That's my son!"

In that moment, time seemed to stand still. Out of the all the keynotes I've given across the country, out of all the casino companies in the world, here was Jason's mother—sitting in this very audience. The sheer improbability of this moment took my breath away. Some might call it coincidence, but to me, it felt like something more—a divine orchestration, a moment meant to be. In an industry built on odds and chance, this connection defied all probability. It was as if Jason's story had drawn us together, completing a circle I never knew needed closing.

I froze. I had never met her before, and I wasn't sure how she would react to hearing me talk about her son, especially given the tragic circumstances of his passing. For a moment, I was paralyzed, unsure of how to proceed.

Gathering my courage, I asked for her permission to continue. To my relief, she nodded, encouraging me to go on. With her blessing, I finished Jason's story, sharing how his positive attitude and genuine appreciation for others had left an indelible mark on me and countless others.

After the speech, Jason's mother approached me. We talked for a long time, and she shared something that I'll never forget. She told me that she had always known Jason loved his job, but hearing my story helped her realize the true impact he had on the people around him. It gave her a new perspective on why he had been so passionate about his work.

"I knew he enjoyed his job," she said, her eyes glistening with tears, "but now I understand that what he really loved was making a difference in people's lives."

This encounter drove home to me the true power of positive leadership. Jason may not have had a fancy title or a corner office, but through his everyday actions, he embodied the very essence of what it means to be a positive leader. He created a ripple effect of positivity that continued long after he was gone, touching lives in ways he probably never imagined.

As leaders, we often focus on metrics like productivity, profitability, and market share. But Jason's story reminds us that our most significant impact often comes from how we make people feel—how we help inflate and sustain the invisible balloons of confidence, potential, and well-being that each person carries. Our actions affect our team members, our customers, and everyone we interact with in ways that extend far beyond any single moment.

Positive leadership isn't just about achieving business goals (although it certainly helps with that). It's about creating an environment where people can thrive, where they feel valued and appreciated, where they're empowered to make a difference. It's about recognizing the humanity in our work and in our workplaces, and understanding that each interaction has the power to either lift someone up or let them down.

When we lead with positivity—when we take the time to say, "Thanks for coming in today," when we celebrate our team's successes, when we trust and empower our people—we create a ripple effect that extends far beyond the walls of our organizations. We touch lives, shape careers, and sometimes, as in Jason's case, leave a legacy that continues to inspire long after we're gone.

As you move forward in your leadership journey, I encourage you to think about the impact you want to have. How do you want your team members to feel when they come to work each day? What kind of environment do you want to create? What legacy do you want to leave?

Positive leadership isn't about grand gestures or elaborate programs. It starts with small, everyday actions—a word of appreciation, a moment of genuine connection, a display of trust and empowerment. These small acts, consistently performed, can transform your team, your organization, and ultimately, the lives of everyone you touch.

My friendship with Jason's mother continues to this day, a beautiful and unexpected outcome of a tragic event. It serves as a constant reminder to me of the far-reaching impact we can have as leaders, often in ways we may never fully realize.

So, as we conclude, I challenge you to embrace the principles of positive leadership we've explored in this book. Start each day with gratitude and appreciation for your team. Look for opportunities to inflate rather than deflate the spirits of those around you. Celebrate the wins, both big and small. Empower your people to make decisions and take ownership. Lead with empathy, trust, and positivity.

And who knows? Maybe someday, someone will tell a story about how your leadership touched their life, about how you helped lift them up when they needed it most, or made a difference in ways you never imagined. That, I believe, is the true measure of a positive leader.

Before we go, I want to encourage you to think about one final question: When people reflect on your leadership years from now, what impact do you hope they'll say you had on their lives? Now, as honestly as you can, ask yourself what changes you need to make today to create that legacy.

Thank you for coming on this journey with me. Now, go out there and lead positively—you never know whose life you might change.

ACKNOWLEDGMENTS

Leadership is never a solo journey. It's built through experiences, mentorship, and the countless individuals who shape us along the way. As I reflect on my path, I'm filled with gratitude for those who helped form the foundation of my leadership philosophy.

First, to the teams I've had the privilege of leading—your dedication, resilience, and willingness to embrace positive change has been inspiring. You sacrificed countless holidays, weekends, and family moments to serve our guests and support each other. Your commitment to excellence, even during the most challenging times, has taught me more about leadership than any book or seminar ever could.

I've been fortunate to learn from some extraordinary leaders throughout my career. A special thank you to Stephanie Schenking, Brian Perkins, Allison Beckner, and Ben Perelmuter—your examples of positive leadership have been instrumental in shaping my approach.

I must also acknowledge the less-than-stellar leaders I've encountered along the way. Your examples taught me what not to do and strengthened my resolve to lead differently. Every challenging experience helped clarify my vision of positive leadership.

To my industry colleagues who've become friends—thank you for the countless conversations, shared insights, and mutual support as we've worked to elevate leadership in hospitality. Your collaboration and willingness to share both successes and failures have enriched my understanding of what great leadership looks like.

To the housekeepers, front desk agents, maintenance workers, servers, and countless other team members who've shared their stories, challenges, and triumphs with me—you've taught me the true meaning of resilience, dedication, and the importance of leading from the heart.

Finally, to my family, who has supported this journey and understood the demanding nature of hospitality leadership—your love and encouragement have made everything possible. Your patience during long hours, missed events, and work emergencies has not gone unnoticed or unappreciated.

To everyone who has been part of this journey—whether for a moment or for years—I want to say what Jason taught me to say many years ago, the simple phrase that changed my perspective on leadership forever: Thanks for coming in today. Your presence, your dedication, and your willingness to be part of this story have made all the difference. Each of you has helped create a ripple of positive change that continues to touch lives far beyond what any of us might have imagined.

ABOUT THE AUTHOR

Ryan Minton is a best-selling author, keynote speaker, and people-first leader who transformed his first job at a hotel front desk into a remarkable journey to senior vice president—proof that great careers can start with a simple welcome and a smile. With over twenty years in hospitality, Ryan climbed every rung of the operational ladder, from checking in guests to managing flagship properties as a general manager, before leading world-class brands including Hilton, Marriott, and IHG as senior vice president.

On a mission to improve the frontline employee experience worldwide, Ryan inspires the leaders who manage teams every day. He developed the Thanks for Coming In Today® principles—a framework for creating workplaces where employees thrive and customer service comes alive. Ryan's hands-on experience fuels his passionate approach: making work life better for frontline teams and the leaders who guide them.

Known for combining practical wisdom with engaging storytelling, Ryan has become one of the most sought-after voices in leadership and employee experience. His insights have been featured in *Forbes, Newsweek,* and across major television networks including CBS, NBC, ABC, and FOX.

Internationally recognized by Global Gurus as one of the World's Best Speakers in both Hospitality and Customer Experience categories, Ryan brings the same energy to the stage that once made him a standout leader in hotel operations.

As a member of the Forbes Business Council and expert contributor to industry publications, Ryan continues to champion the importance of inspired leadership and engaged teams. His approach has helped countless organizations transform their culture from the ground up—because he believes great service starts with serving your team first.

A proud graduate of Miami University, Ryan spent most of his life in Cincinnati (where his heart still beats for the Reds and Bengals) before trading snow for sunshine in South Florida. When he's not energizing audiences with his dynamic keynotes, you can find him on another adventure with his wife Tressa and their son Charlie.

Let's connect!

ryan@ryanminton.com | ryanminton.com

LET'S MAKE 'UPLIFTED' COME ALIVE AT YOUR EVENT

The principles of being "Uplifted" aren't just words on a page—they come to life through genuine human connection! I love delivering humorous, heartfelt keynotes and workshops that transform insights into actionable strategies for your team. Each year, I accept approximately 50 in-person speaking invitations, plus virtual sessions for organizations seeking breakthrough results. My approach combines practical wisdom with memorable storytelling that resonates long after the event ends. Ready to bring these concepts to your team or organization? Learn more about booking possibilities at ryanminton. com/keynote-speaking.